Bogi Bjarnason
... his words

COMPILED BY
BRIAN BJARNASON AND KATE JARVIS

Canadian Cataloguing in Publication Data

Bjarnason, Bogi, 1888–1977.
Bogi Bjarnason ... his words

ISBN   1-894694-06-6

I. Title.
PS8503.J34A6   2001   C818'.5209   C2001-902617-X
PR9199.3.B463A6   200

Researcher and editor: Kate Jarvis
Proofreader: Bernard Shalka
Book design: Fiona Raven
Photo credits: Bogi's memorabilia
provided by his son, Brian Bjarnason
Cover background photo: Rusty MacDonald
with kind permission of his Estate
Cover aircraft drawing: Gordon Clover

First printing October 2001

Creative Connections Publishing
Suite 212 - 1656 Duranleau Street • Granville Island
• Vancouver, B.C. V6H 3S4 • 604-688-0320 •
email: ccpublishing@axion.net
www.creativeconnectionspublishing.com

Affiliated Publishers in
Vancouver • Calgary • Milwaukee • Denver

Printed in Canada

TABLE OF CONTENTS

PREFACE

When my father died and Mother moved to a smaller place, I found myself in possession of a large number of heavy cardboard boxes. These boxes contained scrapbooks filled with samples of my father's writing. They had undoubtedly at one time been reasonably neat and organized as he was usually quite meticulous about things. But in his final few years he very likely moved things around from one file to another, and from one box to another, so there was no order to anything. I finally got them all sorted out and after a delay of a number of years decided that I should publish a collection of some of his editorials, his "Letters from the Front," and some of his miscellaneous writings.

Father was born and attended school in North Dakota. At that time, rural schools went to Grade Eight at the very most and were in session for only short portions of the year, so if you were going to get a well-rounded education it was necessary that you do most of it yourself by building on the limited school curriculum. I have my father's certificates from a Business College in Winnipeg and from a Music Academy in Minneapolis but have been unable to find any reference to any other school or college. From this I assume that his knowledge of literature and his writing skills were self-taught.

Nor have I been able to discover any record of formal religious training and, as he did not hold much brief for any of the churches, can only assume that his thorough knowledge of the Bible stemmed from his admiration of it as a piece of literature. This familiarity seems to have been acquired prior to his military service since he refers to various passages from the Bible in his "Letters from the Front."

My older brother and sister were born in Wynyard, Saskatchewan, and I arrived on the scene some eight years later in Treherne, Manitoba. Both Don and Bernice pursued careers in social work while I took my father's advice and spent thirty-eight years as a pilot with Trans Canada Airlines and then Air Canada. I'm sorry that I did not get this put together in time for Don to see it. He passed away in 1996.

As for the writing samples chosen for inclusion in this book, I have had to be quite selective in my choices of his editorials, endeavouring to reflect the tenor of the times in which they were written. In many cases it would require only a change of names and addition of a number of zeroes to the figures to have them fit right onto the editorial pages of today. Some things do not change all that much. Also included are those that predict the future of aviation, radio, and television, and the one which calls for regulations restricting drinking and driving. Most of his letters from his military training period and all of the "Letters from the Front" have been included.

A 1923 edition of Webster's Unabridged Dictionary was his second "Bible," so the spelling is all in the American format. I have left the spelling and punctuation pretty much as he used them. Even though they seem old-fashioned to us, they give his writing a flavour of the times.

My motive for compiling this book is that I have long admired my father's writing skill, his clear vision of the future, and his acceptance of the many foibles of his fellow human beings. I hope that these writings will convey some of the man he was to those who have, regrettably, never met him. If not in person, then maybe through his own words.

— Brian Bjarnason

I would like to thank Kate Jarvis, who gave this book its form and structure. Her help was invaluable in finding the expertise required to get the book published in this wired world of ours.

BIOGRAPHY

Bjarni Bjarnason and Groa Jonsdottir emigrated from Iceland in the early 1880s. They established a homestead in the small settlement of Mountain, North Dakota, where, for the next forty years, they farmed. Helgi Finnbogi Bjarnason, known as Bogi, was born on September 26, 1888. He was Bjarni and Groa's sixth child.

Bogi was educated at South Dakota School No. 69. In 1910, he moved to St. Paul, Minnesota, to attend school for a year and study the violin. In approximately 1911, he moved to Winnipeg to attend a College of Business, graduating with diplomas in commercial law, rapid arithmetic and correspondence, and junior bookkeeping.

In 1913, Bogi returned to Mountain, North Dakota, to a job as manager of a general implements business. He subsequently moved to Wynyard, Saskatchewan and took over the *Wynyard Advance* from his brother Paul. He stayed there from 1915 to 1919.

In March 1918, Bogi, still an American citizen, was inducted into the US army. He fought for several different units and saw action in various sectors. During the summer of 1918, he was gassed but recovered enough to return to the front. In October, he was gassed again, this time with chlorine. He convalesced in France and, in December 1918, received an Honourable Discharge from the army.

Following his discharge, Bogi returned to Wynyard. He sold the newspaper and married Haldora Christjanson. In August 1919, they moved to Foam Lake, Saskatchewan, where Bogi took over the *Western Review*. In 1922, the couple moved to Kelvington, Saskatchewan. Bogi founded a local newspaper called the *Kelvington Radio*, so named because of his fascination with that new medium. He sold the newspaper in 1927 and moved the family to Winnipeg, Manitoba, where he was the publisher of two Icelandic newspapers, the *Logberg* and the *Heimskringla*.

By the late 1920s, Bogi was concerned about the growing financial crisis spreading across the country. Convinced that the city was a poor place to be during a depression, he and Haldora moved the family, which now included two children, to Treherne, Manitoba, and purchased the *Treherne Times*. Shortly after their arrival, another son was born. Bogi spent the next fifteen years publishing and writing for the *Treherne Times*.

During the early 1930s, Bogi began to develop a fascination with airplanes. Wishing to be a pilot, he took flying lessons in Brandon, Manitoba. In 1933, he bought himself a Pietenpol aircraft, a kit aircraft powered by a modified Ford "Model A" engine. He obtained his pilot's license in 1937, which allowed him to transport passengers.

In 1945, Bogi sold the *Treherne Times* and moved the family to Vancouver. His plan to work for a newspaper was never realized because, after a lifetime of self-employment, he was unsuited to the rigid demands of unions and large publishing firms. So, at the age of 57, he settled into retirement. He continued to write, occasionally for publication, but otherwise for pleasure. He also maintained an active correspondence with friends across the continent.

Bogi Bjarnason passed away in Vancouver, in 1977.

Original home in North Dakota.

BOGI BJARNASON'S FAMILY TREE

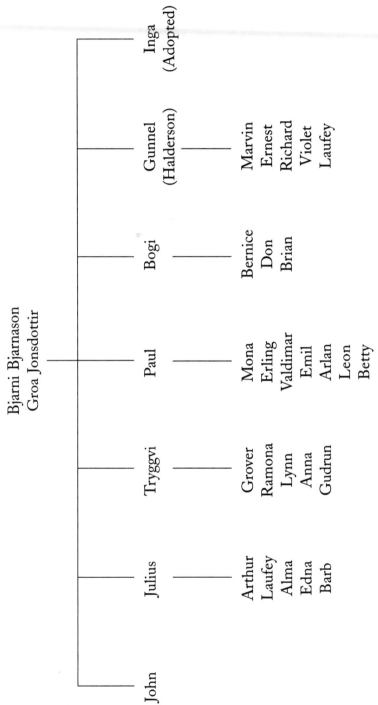

Bjarni Bjarnason
Groa Jonsdottir

John

Julius — Arthur, Laufey, Alma, Edna, Barb

Tryggvi — Grover, Ramona, Lynn, Anna, Gudrun

Paul — Mona, Erling, Valdimar, Emil, Arlan, Leon, Betty

Bogi — Bernice, Don, Brian

Gunnel (Halderson) — Marvin, Ernest, Richard, Violet, Laufey

Inga (Adopted)

HALDORA CHRISTJANSON'S FAMILY TREE

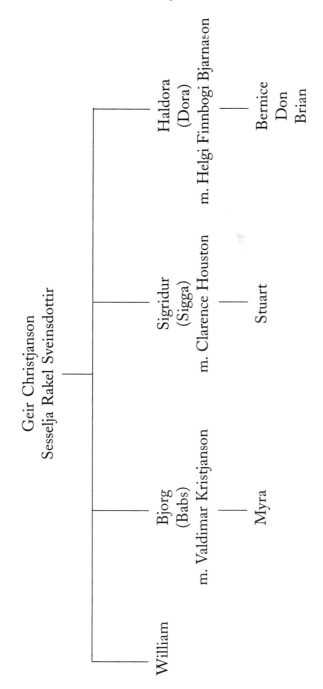

Geir Christjanson
Sesselja Rakel Sveinsdottir

Bjorg
(Babs)
m. Valdimar Kristjanson

Myra

William

Sigridur
(Sigga)
m. Clarence Houston

Stuart

Haldora
(Dora)
m. Helgi Finnbogi Bjarnason

Bernice
Don
Brian

Particulars

FULL NAME   **BOGI BJARNASON**

ADDRESS   **TREHERNE, MANITOBA, CANADA**

TRADE OR OCCUPATION   **PRINTER AND PUBLISHER**

PLACE AND DATE OF BIRTH (WHEN KNOWN)   **MOUNTAIN, NORTH DAKOTA, U.S.A.**

26TH SEPTEMBER 1888

SUBJECT OF CITIZEN   **UNITED STATES**

MARRIED SINGLE WIDOWER (WIDOW)   **MARRIED**

NAME OF WIFE   **(NOT HEREBY NATURALIZED)**

PARENTS SUBJECTS OF CITIZENS   **UNITED STATES**

AGE **48** YEARS   HEIGHT **5** FEET **8½** INCHES

COLOUR **WHITE**   COMPLEXION **RUDDY**

COLOUR OF EYES **GRAY**   COLOUR OF HAIR **DARK**

VISIBLE DISTINGUISHING MARKS **NONE**

COUNTERSIGNED

CHIEF CLERK OF NATURALIZATION

CHAPTER I

WAR DIARIST

Although he had lived in Canada for several years, Bogi Bjarnason was still an American citizen in 1918. Consequently, he was called up by the US army during the last year of World War I. He left Wynyard, Saskatchewan for a boot camp in North Dakota. He was formally inducted into the army on March 29, 1918. Following one month of basic training at Camp Dodge, he joined the North Dakota 35th Regiment.

In April, 1918, the unit was sent to France. Several times over the next month, Bogi was transferred to different regiments. He saw action along the French/German front. In June, he was gassed, but recovered enough to return to the front. In late October of that year, while fighting in the Argonne forest, what he called "my shell — the one with my name, serial number and home address" landed nearby. According to his letters, he had "for some time been listening in on shells, but so far had failed to detect anything personal in their hiss. This particular one fairly called my name, and from the first I knew it was the one." That shell contained deadly chlorine gas.

Bogi spent almost six weeks in a French hospital, recovering. In December, he was shipped to New York aboard the White Star liner *Kroonland*. In late December he was given an Honourable Discharge from the army and returned home to Wynyard.

During and following the war, Bogi wrote three series of articles about the war, all for publication. Some of the articles are addressed to his brother Paul, who was running the *Wynard Advance* in his absence. The first series, "A Student in Arms," was written during his training at Camp Dodge and details his first experience living under military command. The second series, "Letters from France," is made up of letters addressed to his brother Paul. The third series, "A Soldier's Diary," provides a detailed account of Bogi's last month of active duty.

There have been comments made that his writing seems very mature for a "buck private" in Pershing's army. Since he was born in 1888 he was 29 when he was called up, and had been involved in the newspaper business for several years.

A glossary of terms is provided on page 46 at the end of this chapter.

"A STUDENT IN ARMS"

When it came to my mind to write this article and the ones that are to follow, the above heading suggested itself at once. It is satisfactory in this respect, in that I hope to be a student whether in arms or not, nor have I any higher ambition -- to go to school to every man I meet, to bow to and salute my elders in the gentle art of living, and never to graduate.

On the other hand, I have no desire to try to do badly what Hankey -- requiescat in pace -- has done so splendidly. His ready understanding and facile pen have almost hallowed the phrase, and for one so unworthy as the writer to attempt to assume his mantle is preposterous. His the fire and the grace of expression so sadly lacking in these notes; yet the theme will be along close lines: a student's impressions of his fellows under military discipline, the individual and the collection, and that must serve as the reason for impressing Hankey's title into further service as a text.

*　　*　　*

The days of heroics are over. The "glory of war" is forever dispelled, nor must it ever again be allowed to rear its head. It is a pleasant picture to associate with the knights-errant of old, who were always freeing distressed damsels; but the sordidness of modern warfare has discounted the glory and left heroics to the dime-novelist. That is the reason Tennyson's song of the charge at Balaclava has been superseded by "Tip-perary."

Yet the Crusaders or Vikings of old have no examples of heroism to their credit that cannot be duplicated by those unassuming heroes who are staying the Hun hordes as we write. And the heroism of today is in this respect much the grander that it is unassuming, almost unconscious. But the trumpet is silent and must remain silent.

Because of this new order the Student cannot feel the exultation of the call to arms, but sets out humming his merry tune, without a thought of "the shining sword" and other impedimenta. In his packsack he has a copy of the St. James version of The Book, between the leaves of which a fine tooth comb is doing service as a bookmark; nor is there any feeling of levity in the placing of it. To offset the heaviness of the matter the Rubaiyat is also taken along. The Latin Syntax will have to wait better times.

Thus equipped the Student sets forth, with a cheerful Au Revoir to all his well-wishers.

The Student.

*   *   *

The formal ceremony of inducting the county's contingent began at ten in the morning and lasted until three in the afternoon, the time being occupied with speeches, singing and prayer, not to mention parades and the posing for photographs. Two brass bands, their silver horns gleaming in the sun, dispensed martial music in lieu of war paint...

...Said this morning when the blast for "Reveille" sounded: "It doesn't take long to spend a night in the army." No one laughed. One is not in the mood for laughing at five in the morning if one has to get up and a hard day is ahead...

During the first six months of mobilization no less than 90 per thousand soldiers contracted venereal diseases. (Measles come second among the other diseases with 20 per thousand. Typhoid, that ancient scourge, brought up the rear, accounting for 1/57 of one per cent, due no doubt to the inoculation.) Hordes of vampires in human form followed in the wake of the army soliciting the soldiers, and this, of course, was the source of contagion. Harsh measures were taken, first with the women and later with the diseased soldiers, in an effort to lessen the evil, but as this is not thoroughly effective, the chivalry of the men is being appealed to. Lectures are given on hygiene, the pivots of these being an appeal to the men to maintain self-respect...

Militarism in America has come to stay. There is absolutely no question about it. The large and boasted freedom of the United States citizen is in abeyance, and will be held there. So while the western democracies are fighting to crush German militarism, they are building up a militarism at home even more formidable, and which eventually will turn and rend them...

... These are not the poet's soldiers, who burn with inward fire, egged on by the cause of Galahads seeking the Holy Grail, swearing fearful oaths. They are prosaic, matter-of-fact. They may change when up against the real thing, but among the different classes in America today the War is of less concern to the soldier than to anyone else. A good many of them have not been able to make much of a

Bogi in field uniform, 1918.

fist of life, so death has small terrors. The more immediate cause is the attitude of the officers, who lose no opportunity of impressing upon the men the cheapness of human life. What boots it if this or that grain of sand is lost? The avalanche moves relentlessly on.--

"The eternal Saki from his bowl has poured
Millions of bubbles like us, and will pour."

*   *   *

...Just a word about the benevolent organizations, such as the Red Cross and the Y.M.C.A. To these I would say, keep up the great, good work! I could name nothing quite so worthy of support as the Red Cross. Although the men are supplied with the direst necessities by the government, the little comforts are sadly and conspicuously lacking, and the soldier has but meagre opportunities of obtaining them, even when the wherewithal is at hand. These little com-

Parade Uniform, 1918.

forts are not wholly necessary. Indeed they are more vital than a civilian living in comfort can fully appreciate. These big boys are not sufficient unto themselves, and a good many are babes in the wood, heart hungry, lonesome children, to whom any solicitude shown finds ready appreciation. And to those who have found time and inclination to write to boys at the front or at the cantonments, I would say, keep it up! A letter from home is even as a sudden burst of sunshine on a dreary day...

The big guns are booming on the range north of camp. They are not big, of course, being three and five inch field pieces only, and would look small beside their seventeen inch grown-up brothers in Europe; but to us of the plains, they look and act "big" enough. Indeed they do. And vindictive! Their barking is voluminous -- loud and heavy, and the note of Power is manifest.

But above and through the reverberations comes the hiss of spite, the expressed desire to tear and rend. Truly theirs is the anthem of hate. It is unmistakable. Cannon are not made to sow or reap with, or assist in any of the arts. Man-made engines of destruction, their voices are so singularly free from hypocrisy. Their rage is elemental; it is their breath of life. Their vengeful rumblings are the suspirations of incarnate human hate.

"LETTERS FROM FRANCE"

Undated

Dear Paul:

Am writing this prone on the grass in an orchard in "Sunny France" with the larks singing bravely overhead, undaunted by those monstrous guns which keep incessantly belching hard by, nor by the answering shells. The day is lovely, as every day here is lovely, and one cannot help marveling that human strife is possible in such surroundings. Nature seems so glad and responsive when petted by the hand of the tiller and so ready to yield forth her fruits, that the heart is touched with a gentleness of kinship and brotherliness. The cattle that bask and chew their cud in the sun, speak of a peace and contentment so out of keeping with what is going on about them, that a rose budding in a field of glaciers could hardly be more incongruous. I could imagine no greater contrast than the sweet serenity of the orchard where I lie, and the raging inferno of war within easy shelling range.

But if it seems almost sacrilegious to hurl shells at and raze those ancient castles, as we see about us, if these orchards became caldrons of hell, seething with the rage of men, that does not excite pity, as does the sight of the Children of France. These melt the heart. On these, indeed, Mars lays a heavy hand, crushing body and spirit, inflexibly and relentlessly.

By the term, Children of France, I refer not only to the young, who in these parts, have not suffered so much; I refer to the children of sixty and up, the gentle mothers who have seen their idols go forth only to return maimed and broken or else not at all; the tearless fathers who shake impotent fists at the inflamed sky -- these, these stir our pity. To see them in the fields bending over their clumsy tools from early morn till the gathering dusk enfolds them, in a brave effort to "carry the packs" of the fallen, must steel the heart of all who see to a determination that this frightful thing called war shall never again be unloosed. For it is not upon the warrior that the heaviest burden is laid, but upon those who love him and yet can do so little for him. To die bravely is less hard than to live bravely; and if the Poilu is brave, the little mother, or wife, or sweetheart who sent him forth to do battle against the forces of darkness is no less brave.

The little mother where we are billeted, whose two fine sons have now given their all; her infirm mother, the two youngest, nine and eleven, and mademoiselle Nineteen in her hobnailed shoes -- these have not escaped. As she pours out wine for us, she tells us, or tries to, that we are like her two boys.

There are no tears. These are confined to the pillow; but at times there is a note of bitterness at the injustice of this cruel thing that robbed her of her dearest possession. A shell may at any time fall upon the thatched roof of her little hut, but this has no terror for her. She shrugs her little shoulders:

Of what worth is life now?

Do not look for any word of what we are doing. It is all so fast and furious, that were I allowed to give my impressions of frontier life, I could not do it. The soldier knows very little of what is taking place outside his horizon, and when stories are passed from mouth to mouth, as they constantly are, they are generally greatly exaggerated when not wholly "black crows." But I find the life less irksome than I had been led to think, and if a large part of our work is "fatigue" it is not all colorless. The uncertainty lends zest, and when "iron foundries" are running amuck and the earth trembles with their impact, the moments are not all drab. So if we have not all the comforts of home, I cannot wholly envy you, for there are some things which must be lived to be understood, and those of us who return will be enriched in some ways if impoverished in others.

*   *   *

May 26, 1918

Dear Paul:

Have been transferred again, this time to a crack, trained regiment, but shall not now give its name, so that if I do say something about myself, I shall betray no secrets. It can certainly be of no military importance to the enemy to know that I am but a few miles to the rear of the first line trenches, even if this letter happens to fall into his hands. And the censor, being a man of intelligence, will readily understand this.

As I write, the guns are booming their wrath and at night the sky is lit up with star shells. We have our gas masks on our breast continually and our rifles are within reach at all times. By the time this reaches you I shall have seen action and come to grips with the enemy. That's what we are here for.

Just two months ago I left Wynyard and one month ago left Camp Dodge. How does that compare with the speechifying patriots back home?

Were someone going to ask me how I felt about going into battle, I would very probably not be able to say a word. I am tense with a curious mixture of abandon and anxiety, but feel anything but afraid. This method of warfare does not allow of that. Bayonet drill is the unpleasantest part.

Am now alone of all the boys who set out from Cavalier [a small town in North Dakota]. A good many succumbed to the rigors of the journey and are scattered in hospitals along the way. All the Icelanders who came over with me on the boat are in hospitals. It was a very trying voyage and many gave in, the strong and healthy as quickly as the rest. Marching with packs weighing a hundred pounds does test one severely. At one time we were on the go for thirty-two hours and during that time we had but one light lunch of hardtack and coffee. Oh, Sherman said it!

But as a rule we get enough to eat and are treated well. Of course the work is hard; but then we are on no holiday.

*　　*　　*

Somewhere in France, June 28th, 1918

Dear Paul:

Am writing this in an honest to goodness American hospital, in an institution that would put to shame many good hospitals back home. We are housed in a building on a par with the Royal Alex at Winnipeg, so that discomforts are nil and we want nothing, except mail from home. I, for one, have ceased to look for it. We are four in a ward, gas patients, none of us very sick, so time doesn't press, and I am enjoying my first real rest in a long time.

Well, I have been "up," meaning to the lines, and though I have not seen the whites of the enemy's eyes, I have seen enough to get a thorough dislike for him and his ways. You will remember that I used to say that one side was rarely white and the other black when a quarrel was on, and that probably this was a war of capitalism and all that junk. Well, I'm converted now. I've seen some of his work, and the more I see, the less I like him. A close up view is not the same as one from a distance of six thousand miles; and if he has shown his character any-where, it is in France.

He is mad, stark mad. No civilized, rational mind could have brought this about. But as with Hamlet, "there is method in his madness," and one cannot quell a sneaking admiration for his unquestioned efficiency. No one can come to grips with him and not gain respect for him as a fighter. He thinks out things and then does them by rote; and if he is a slow and moderately bright thinker, he is methodical and thorough, and damned efficient.

Take his manner of gassing, for instance. He will send over some evil-smelling stuff to deaden your senses, followed by the colorless, deadly gas. And once a whiff of that gets you, you are "out of luck," as the boys say. And on calm days a shrapnel shell will immediately follow the gas shell to distribute the vapor, and almost invariably it finds the very hole where the gas shell burst.

* * *

New York City, December 12, 1918

Dear Paul:

Docked yesterday morning on our fifteenth day out from St. Nazaire, our ship being the White Star Liner Kroonland, 13,000 tons net. The passage was exceptionally rough through-out, the roughest in the experience of the crew; and when a sailor admits that the sea is disturbed, his word can be taken without discount.

Off the Newfoundland banks we ran into a hurricane of great severity. The ship's instruments recorded a pressure of sixty miles an hour, and this intensity kept for over ten hours. I recalled a phrase from Jacobs about the sea being "lashed into fury," and then and there I realized that the phrase was an apt one, for a rough sea gives a very distinct impression of rage. It is more than disturbed, it is angry.

The ship left her course and stood into the wind, barely holding her own under full steam. Monstrous, mountainous swells swept her from bow to stern, carrying off everything breakable on deck, including lockers, and even lookout cages and rafts were smashed on the promenade deck. The covering was blown off a hatchway and the bulkhead shipped three feet of water before this could be replaced, which proved to be a very hazardous task.

Every oncoming swell seemed greater than the preceding one, and as the ship met the impact her bow went under, only to rear up as she slid into the trough, where she would quiver like the striking arrow. At times it seemed as if she must go to pieces before such terrible battering, but no important rivet gave. The chief danger at such times is injury to the rudder, upon which the strain is multiplied, and to the screws, which are alternately sawing the air or churning the water at an increased depth and pressure. The rudderless ship of course is doomed, as broadside to such swells would soon reduce the staunchest chest to splinters.

I felt easy, with the confidence of the ignorant, until I heard two of the crew in whispered consultation, after which I wished earnestly for "Blutcher or night." The sea is hospitable, they say, but somehow it looked cold and the thought of a raft was not cheering, -- the less so as I contemplated that tins of "bully beef" are tied to the rafts for the sustenance of the unfortunate, and I am off of that for life. That I had succeeded in ducking umpty-million machine gun bullets and half as many large shells in the Argonne, and all the "Minnenwerfers" at Metzeral, so I felt that this wasn't due me. But the two sailors had spoken of "when" she founders and not "if," as if that were inevitable. But she came through (bless her creaky heart), and here I am, in "lil ole New Yawk" none the worse but a lot wiser. -- I shall never run away to sea -- Never! If the Statue of Liberty ever wishes to see me again it will have to make an "about face."

Am here at a debarkation camp waiting to be mustered out. Fear that I cannot be with you Xmas, but in any case it will not be very long now. Meanwhile, best of luck.

Mid-Atlantic, early Dec., 1918; New York-bound from Brest.
Wind-force 60m., n.n.w.

THE KROONLAND
DAILY WIRELESS

"LAY DOWN YOUR ARMS."

Issued Daily on
Return Trip

Price—2 Cents

Volume I   SUNDAY   Number 7

ARMY OF OCCUPATION TO BE BROUGHT HOME BY SUMMER

Eight of the thirteen divisions of the third army now on German soil approaching the Rhine are either national guard or national army troops and there is every reason to believe that they will be on American soil by mid-summer. General March announced today he anticipated no difficulty in getting these units home within four months after peace is formally established by proclamation. The army of occupation is increased by five divisions which are located in Luxemberg. Nine million pounds of candy for the army has just been ordered by the war department it is announced today. A considerable part is to be rushed overseas to insure a plentiful supply for Christmas.

On Board The U. S. S. George Washington

The President's ship today ran through a severe wind and rain storm. It is maintaining fixed speed, however and is due to pass around the Azores Sunday. Then they will pick up more units of the naval escort. The President slept until late this morning and there was no conference with his advisors. The resignation of Charles M. Schwab as director general of the emergency fleet corporation has been accepted by the President in a wireless from the George Washington. Bernard Baruch and Henry P. David-son have been asked by the President to hold themselves in readiness to respond to call for their services with the peace delegation in Europe. It is understood advice will be needed in the work of feeding and rehabilitating the destitute nations.

The United States navy will total twelve hundred and ninety one ships, including forty battleships and three hundred and twenty nine destroyers July first, 1920, according to Admiral Griffins statement to the House Naval Affairs committee today. Admiral Taylor told the committee of contracts yet to be placed for twenty nine ships which have been authorized. Work has not started on five battle cruisers authorized in 1916.

The New York stock market continued the move on narrow lines, trading being entirely professional, public interest for a time being eliminated. Most of action was in industrial groups, rails still dragging with fractional changes. Action in steel common increased as session advanced and Bethlehem gained a point.

Minstrel Show Enjoyed by Crew.

Last night the minstrel show was repeated in the Troop's Mess Hall, for members of the crew. It was again a Big Success. Enough credit cannot be given to Mr. Lerner for his untiring efforts in coaching the members of the cast, the result of which was an evening of pleasure for all concerned.

THE SHIPS
By Theodore Maynard

The bending sails shall whiten on the
    sea,
    Guided by hands and eyes made
    glad for home,
With graven gems and cedar and
    ebony
    From Babylon and Rome.
For here a lover cometh as to his bride,
    And there a merchant to his utmost
    price—
Oh, hearts will leap to see the ships
    ride
    Safety to Paradise!
And this that cuts the waves with
    brazen prow
    Hath heard the blizzard groaning
    through her spars;
Battered with honor swings she nobly
    now
    Back from her bitter wars.
And that doth bring her silver work
    and spice,
    Peacocks and apes from Tarshish,
    and from Tyre,
Great cloaks of velvet stiff with gold
    device,
    Colored with sunset fire. . . . . .
And one, serenely through the golden
    gate,
    Shall sail and anchor by the ulti-
    mate shore,
Who, plundered of her gold by pirate
    Fate,
    Still keeps her richer store.
Unrifled when her perilous journey
    ends
    And the strong cable holds her safe
    again:
Laughter and memories and the songs
    of friends
    And the sword-edge of pain.

THE KROONLAND DAILY WIRELESS.

NAUTICAL CATECHISM.
Chapter IV.

Who is the officer-in-charge?

The officer-in-charge is the solemn, bored-looking man, usually attired in some nondescript uniform, who, at times may be found slowly pacing one side of the bridge. He is supposed to direct the firing in case of an attack upon the ship. Before the war, he was selected for his great knowledge or lack of any knowledge, about gunfire. No middle ground was permitted. Now, he is selected for his wide experience in the handling of ships. Often this experience is so wide that it has become far-fetched and we find that the officer-in-charge has forgotten more than he ever knew. When the officer-of-the-deck makes a good move, the officer-in-charge takes the credit; when the O. O. D. makes a mistake, does the officer-in-charge take the blame? You bet, he does.-not! When the officer-in-charge is in good humor, he tells youthful O. O. D's and Jr. O. O. D's about the intricacies of the rules of the road and the wonders of the heavenly bodies, including Venus. When his liver is in bad shape, he speaks not a word, growls at intervals and swears when someone approaches him, with the question, "Officer-of-the-Deck? (This inspite of his disguise). Before he can deny that he is, the words follow, "I want pressure on the deck pump" or something else which the poor Officer-in-charge knows nothing about. In fact, he is totally oblivious of everything that is going on about the ship. When the Officer- in - charge becomes too bored or too tired of being asked foolish questions, he retires to the Chart Room and there reads a thrilling novel, such as. "The Navigator's Revenge or Who Stole The Chart"; or communes with Morpheus, which is more often the case.

THE MISTERY OF A KNOX HAT
(A True Story)
By E. Conan Chambers.

He was neither tall nor short. His appearance was not striking. But he wore spats and carried a cane, which made him a well-dressed man, on Fifth Avenue. As he sauntered gaily into The Big Book Store, he failed to attract more than the usual attention accorded a book parasite. He followed the ordinary routine, i. e. priced a set of expensive books, ordered some stationary sent to a fictitious address, jabbered in French to the lady in the foreign dept, and asked for a rare edition, which could only be purchased with considerable trouble. "But they would get it for him from their branch in Paris." "No, they needn't bother, he was sailing for Europe in a few days and no doubt would be able to secure it himself." Then he settled down to wandering among the various alcoves.

(To be continued)

SUBTLE SOLILOQUIES.

Marriage is a contract in which there is seldom a "Meeting of the minds"—Note;—In a "Real" contract, there must be a "Meeting of the minds" of the two parties concerned. This is our own work, so don't pick it apart.

The papers said that "Gumshoe Bill" had died. But he left many a namesake. There are "Gumshoe Bills" in every age and clime, even on board ships of the Navy, but they soon lie low on board ships of the Navy.

On account of the war, "they're wearin 'em STILL higher in Hawaii." "By golly", we wish we were back there, far from these wintry blasts, underneath those sheltering pineapple trees, with that same old "Book of verse, flask of wine, loaf of bread, and Thou."

Requests are the order of the day,
No more do I want Navy pay
To land a job, is what I pray;
Oh, Captain, please don't say me nay!
My folks? They need me, sure they do,
Aw, be a sport. It's up to you
"I want to go home."
Ima Gob.

"Break, break, break, on thy cold grey stones, O sea!
And I would that my tongue could utter the thoughts that arise in me."

If you were the Editor of this paper, it could.

A MATTER OF NECESSITY

She (pouting) —I believe you would sooner play cards with papa than sit in the parlor with me.

He—No, darling, I wouldn't; but we must have the money to get married on.

Bound Copies of "THE DAILY WIRELESS"
Issued During This Trip
Will Be Sold on the Day
Of Arrival In Port.

"A SOLDIER'S DIARIES"

(Written in the first line of trenches opposing the Germans on Kiosk Hill, in the German Vosges, Alsace, half a kilometre above Metzeral. Time 5:00 a.m.)

Sept. 3rd

On guard. Went on at 7 last night. If all goes well should be relieved at 7. Cold. Hungry. Was hungry when I went on last night. Have been on sentry duty now for four nights straight, 12 hours per shift. The other 12 hours it is work. Buried Hagerman and Marshall yesterday. What with the two ration details the time allowed for sleep is scant, -- not more than four hours, often less.

The sun is over the Swiss Alps now. Yesterday I saw the Rhine, only 14 miles distant. The valley was then full of clouds below -- cirro cumulus -- Jerry was throwing shells into the cloud mass.

The vigil is over for the night. Jerry doesn't start things at this hour without due warning. We got the customary "evening blessing" last night in the form of "flying pigs" (We call it "strafe," he calls it "blessing"). He throws them from mortars on top of the hill, I wonder if the possessed pigs of old were more demonstrative?

This is called a quiet sector. Quiet hell! Raids every night, back or forth. Last week we penetrated a mile into his preserves, and he never said "boo." Last night but one he tried to come over on us but our emma gees stopped him. Three hours ago he had a patrol out. I saw it. -- But then one sees and hears things here that never were on land or sea. I saw a burly Dutchman in our wires and emptied the magazine at him. When day broke I saw a post. It stood only two feet high at that.

*   *   *

Undated

Christ, the night is long! So fearfully dark and creepy, too. Am all alone since Garvey went "bugs." Kelling is on the right, at least ten rods off. Martin is an equal distance to the left. The guard is "thin" in the first line, which is good strategy. If Jerry comes over the sentries are gone anyway, be they one or a dozen. We are here only to send off the rockets. He knows it too, so he's after us. Getting us alive is good pickins, as we might give information. And of course it's annoying to find the sentries dead every third morning. It makes the men nervous.

I'd give a million, -- nay, a billion dollars would I give, -- for a cup of coffee now. I'd sell my soul for an honest to God meal -- a square feed and time to sleep! Lay down yesterday, and a four pound rat dragged a wet tail across my face, while the cooties formed fours on my back.

Then my night off. At 9 p.m. eleven of us crept into the quarry dug-out. At three Jerry started in with his "blessing." One of his "pigs" landed on the quarry edge. The side of the dug-out came in and the roof came down. Where Corpl. Peters and I slept the beam ends remained in place, the other ends resting on the floor. We decided to leave. Two of the others were found alive, I hear. The rest are decently buried, with cross sticks over their graves, their identification tags slung.

In time the poppies, blood-red and beautiful, will blow on these little, lost mounds .... splendid fellows they were, too. In a way I envy them, for they just beat us to it. Most of us will "Go West" before the thing is over anyway.

*   *   *

(Entered at Kruth, a village in the Alsation Mountains, 6 miles behind the lines.)

Sept. 5th, Evening

My last entry was made on the morning of the third. That day was spent like the rest, carrying rations from the reserve kitchen down to the ruins of Metzeral, where some of our men stay in cellars, and to the sentries on Kiosk Hill. We got the usual "blessing," but this time our batteries answered briskly and with effect. As a rule Jerry throws about six shells to our one.

That evening I was placed on "gas guard" on the promontory behind Metzeral. A powerful klaxon was stationed there to warn our men at the supply dumps, and the reserve at Miftlach, if gas rockets were seen.

Took over the post at seven. At ten a heavy rain set in, lasting till early morning. In half an hour I was wet to the skin for our slickers shed not a drop. In a copy of the "Herald" I stole while on Lieut. R's detail, I saw something about profiteering in army raincoats. (Remarks deleted.)

*   *   *

Undated

At three Jerry started searching for our batteries with his guns back of Kiosk. Ours were at Miftlach, directly back of my post. His shells therefore passed over my head, -- those that didn't fall short. One of our M.G. dug-outs was hit directly. One of the men had no marks on him, the concussion alone killing him. -- A shell made a gaping hole nearby, into which I crept. For a while it was warm and dry. I was exceeding homesick.

*   *   *

Sept. 6th, routine

Went on the same post again at 7. The French were to relieve us this night. Each one received instructions about the route to Kruth, where the company was to reform. At 4 a "Frog" (we have given the French, and anything and everything French this ungainly name) relieved me, and after rolling my pack set out alone. As the crow flies the distance was only six miles. I am not a crow. When day broke I had lost my way and was heading for the lines. I wandered till noon, when I met a Frog who put me on the right track. I made Kruth at two this morning. Tried to rush the kitchen guard and nearly got killed for my pains. Had eaten nothing since 4 p.m. day before yesterday. He was there, he said, to guard the grub, not to give it away, so I went without.

Rolled up in my blanket and shelter -- half in the grass and slept. It rained this morning.

Had three meals today (had only two a day in the trenches), but we never get all we want. This life has its drawbacks.

Three Boche planes tried to raid the town this afternoon and dropped a few bombs. When I heard the first one come whistling down I pulled up my slicker collar. Air bombs are fearful things. They shot down one of the planes. I hear we are moving out tonight.

*   *   *

(Entered at Neuves Maisons, near Nancy. In billets)

Sept. 8th

Last entry made at Kruth. Have since been travelling, arriving here at 10 this a.m. The whole division is stationed here, -- something big is afoot. Everybody senses it.

Left Kruth at 9 p.m. on the 5th. Travelled that night in trucks through the mountains, to Girardmer, I think. Followed winding paths along the mountainside. Cliffs were perpendicular up and down, the road being hewn from the side. No lights were allowed, of course.

Rested during the day at Girardmer. When night fell we were herded into little R.R. vans, the "40 Hommes, 8 cheveau" kind. We were 44 to a car, and of course could not sit or lie down all at once. Under these conditions the men became snarling beasts. A night in one of these is a very trying experience. Of course it was not new to us, for we had spent 72 hours in one from Amiens to Alsace.

I am suffering from trench fever pains in my knees and ankles, especially at night. That night I lay on the floor, with four or five men on top of me. Sleep is out of the question, and I could not move. It wasn't exactly a comfortable night. Some had to stand in the same position all night. To fall on the writhing, cursing mass would probably have meant their lives. There isn't much brotherly love lost aboard these cars.

When day broke we detrained and the company made for a bluff about 2 miles distant, in squads, 50 yards apart. The lines are but a few miles off, and Boche planes might at any moment come over. The bluff reached, we rolled up in our blankets. I slept well despite the rain. We had two meals, -- the usual "slum" and hardtack, at 9 a.m. and 4.

As night fell we slung our packs -- mine weighs 115 pounds -- and set out. All are feeling quite fit. Happy, too, all in all. It isn't exactly a picnic, but then we have nothing to worry about. "Where do we go from here, boys, where do we go from here?" We never know.

We set out at 7 p.m. At 1 a.m. we rested 45 minutes and had hot sweetened coffee, minus the milk. A sandwich would have been welcomed, but that was out of the question. At 10 a.m. this morning we reached here, having made 26 miles. Such hikes really do try the stamina, and quickly weed out the unfit. We are pretty well hardened by now, and the men are standing up well. -- But we could eat a lot more than we get.

As soon as the billet was reached most of the men just

dropped in their tracks and were soon locked in a sleep from which apparently nothing could wake them except the incessant hunger. My usual ill-luck hounded me out and I was put on K. P. (helping in the kitchen).

After rifling a box of hardtack I stole off and slept till supper. I shall probably get guard-duty tonight in consequence.

* * *

Sept. 10th, same place

These last two days have been wonderful, wonderful! Nothing to do, so to speak. We are being fed extra well, and this morning Corp. Long remarked that we were being fattened for slaughter. The officers are constantly lecturing us on open warfare tactics and all are taught the assembling and manipulation of automatic rifles. The feeling is that we will soon have some real work to do.

My platoon commander, though only a "shavetail" (second lieut.), is a gentleman and a capital fellow. Nothing uppish about him like Lieutenant R. He "rides" us and lies awake nights thinking up new ways to torture his men. But he had better look to his life insurance as he'll never die of old age. The Dutch are not going to get him, either. It'll be his own men. If I'm on the scene I'll sure lend a hand. So far the men have had no opportunity. If he goes over with the men he'll never, never come back.

A letter today! The fourth one in as many months. Not from home, either, but from some skirt down in Illinois who has adopted me. Might have been worse -- a "subscription due" notification, for instance.

"C'est la guerre."

* * *

(Entered in a forest; "Somewhere in France.")

Sept. 12th, evening

Shortly before dusk last night got orders to roll our packs. As night fell we lined up in heavy marching order, each carrying 240 rounds of ammunition, and an extra supply of hardtack, bully beef, and water. Numbers 1 and 5 carried the extra water for the squad. I am number 5.

Just as we set out heavy rain begins falling. We all have slickers, but they shed nary a drop. Some firm in the States is making big money on these slickers.

A soldier's uniform and pack are hospitable to water. A blanket rolled up can hold an unbelievable amount of it. It doesn't lighten the burden any, either. I would have sworn I was carrying a ton. But that may be overstating. -- I now have two very dear wishes; -- meeting those raincoat profiteers, and meeting Lieut. R in civilian clothes.

The night was intensely dark, and we were constantly jostling each other. About midnight I had developed a monstrous blister, which added somewhat to the general unpleasantness.

One thing only made the night and the whole business bearable -- a beautiful barrage. Beautiful! I calls it. The Dutch were catching merry hell, and the idea of it was sweet and soothing.

Our guns loosened up about 11 p.m. at the rate of 1400 shells per minute per mile on a thirty mile front, 'twas said. Talk about a hullabaloo! If that couldn't put the fear of God into the heart of the stoutest "Squarehead" that ever walked, nothing on earth could.

Early this morning we were halted, and advised to take what rest we could, but to be ready on two minutes notice. (I learned later that we were to "leap over" the shock troops near the "impregnable" Montsec, but the Germans were so demoralized that the entire St. Mihiel salient caved in and our division took no active part in the push.) Have slept the sleep of the innocent all day, and awhile ago we got word to pitch pup tents and "make ourselves at home" for the night. -- Wish they'd feed us something.

*   *   *

Sept. 16th, same place

This "la guerre" is getting to be a soft snap. Nothing to do all day but work and stand guard at night. Four days of it!

The worst feature is the scarcity of water -- none this side of the Moselle, four miles away. When I'm not on k.p. I'm on "water detail." At night about half the company stands guard over the other half -- to guard them from what is a mystery to me. I am of the half that stands guard.

A wonderful thing happened today. Ran into "Bud" Marble, of Foam Lake! Well, that was one bit of luck alright. We fervently wished ourselves back in God's country, where you didn't need to feed a division of cooties on half rations yourself.

Had another stroke of luck last night that gave me a deal of satisfaction. Was on guard, and as usual got strict injunctions to put out any light. Boche planes might come over at any time and learn our position.

My beat lay past the major's tent. About 11 o'clock a dispatch rider had come up in quest of the major, and having found Lieutenant R the two came on a hunt for the major's tent. Halting them, I made them tell me their life histories, so to speak, and was on the point of turning them away on a technicality, well realizing that I would have to suffer for it all the hardships and indignities of which R. could think on the morrow. At this moment the major came out and the "jig was up."

But on my return beat I spied what I had been hoping against hope for -- the major had lit a tiny candle by which to read and answer the message. A faint glimmer through the side of the tent was visible.

Gods on high. Olympus! A major and his aide caught with the swag. Believe you me, there was one doughboy in Pershing's

23

army whose heart beat high with satisfaction that night. I liked the major -- loved him almost, for his fine qualities -- (a trust not misplaced, for he was later to prove himself as fine a soldier as ever wore a Sam Browne) but here was an opportunity that not often came to a buck private. Pass it up? Nothing doing!

My voice doesn't lend itself readily to issuing commands, but in the three words that first came to me, "douse that light" there was both authority and power. What if the major was reading an important message from Pershing? The light was against regulations.

For one brief moment there was hesitation, then the lieutenant snapped something about my "freshness." I said "I'll give you just fifteen seconds to put it out, or I'll shoot it out!"

The light disappeared, and the dispatch rider came out. The two officers had crept under the blanket with the light, where the major wrote his message.

But I have left to reap the whirlwind.

*   *   *

(Another Forest, "Somewhere in France")

Sept. 20th

What a life this is! No sooner have we grown attached to a place than along comes someone and says, "Get thee hence, for this is not thy rest; take up thy bed and walk."

Day before yesterday, about noon, word came to 'Fall in with packs', and off we swung. After a march of some two hours we came upon the divisional truck train, stretched in a seemingly endless procession as far as the eye could reach. We were assigned 20 to a truck, and what with our packs, not much floor space was left untaken. By crouching some could sit down, but the larger number were "strap hangers."

We lumbered along all afternoon, through Toul, and towards the going down of the sun. Then night fell, and still we kept going till about 4 in the morning. During all of this time I had stood in the same place, so the change to hiking was welcome, even if well-nigh tired out. After a walk of some five hours we reached our present "home" and dug in. Not exactly an inviting place, but 'twill do. The company was assigned to about a quarter acre on an exceedingly steep hill, so we had to dig shelves to keep from rolling down.

After making ready to get some sleep, along comes mess sergeant Radville looking for me -- some of Lieut. R's work, no doubt. But I'll do a lot of fatigue before feeling sorry for having humiliated him. -- Carried water and wood for the kitchen the rest of the day. When at last I "hit the hay" -- minus the hay -- I needed no soothing syrups to go to sleep. Spread out my blanket and shelter-half and rolled up in them on my shelf.

About 2 a.m. I woke up to find that I was lying in a puddle of water, for the shelf was saucer-shaped, and the rain came down in sheets and torrents. Worse, it was cold, and my teeth knocked. There was seemingly no remedy, so I scooped a ditch with my mess tin for the surplus water to keep from drowning. Daylight brought little warmth, so I have spent pleasanter days than this one. But the cooties are having the time of their young lives.

*   *   *

Sept. 24th, same place

Our long range rifles are shooting from the other side of the hill over our heads, and in the general direction of the trenches. As the shells whine in passing I fervently wish some "Squarehead" gets it in the neck. This loving thy neighbor and turning the other cheek is in abeyance.

We're tuning up for something real now. Different officers are constantly lecturing us in tactics -- liquid fire, gas, bayonet, bombing -- Let's go; it can hardly be worse than lying in soak here.

No requisition of clothing yet. Few of us have any under-wear, and socks are in tatters. My toes and knees are out, -- the men are getting hard-boiled -- turning into snarling beasts. Probably that is what the officers want. But the "glory of war" is dispelling.

*   *   *

(In hospital, Langres)

Oct. 1st

Last entry made on the 24th. From then til the evening of the 25th we occupied our holes in the hillside. The days were so drab I had no heart even to record the fact of being alive. Since the evening of the 25th I have been occupied with other things.

During the afternoon of the 25th the company was reorgan-ized and men placed according to their fitness. I was assigned to an ordinary rifle squad, with the post of auxiliary runner. After inspection we were given extra rations and two bombs each. I dislike bombs for their proclivity of going off on the least provocation; and when they go off in your pocket they make such a mess of you. But when well behaved are keen weapons.

Just as dusk fell we were lined up and were addressed by the major. In its way it was a most remarkable speech. This, in effect, is what he said:

"Tomorrow morning at 5:30 we go over the top. Raids car-ried out during the last few days have disclosed the fact that we will be opposed by some of the enemy's best troops. You will therefore have an opportunity of showing your mettle; and you must not fail.

But lest there be any whose determination weakens either before the line is reached or after the 'show' begins a cordon of picked men will see to it that no one drops out, and these have strict orders to dispatch with the bayonet anyone that halts. Should you fall unconscious you are merely out of luck, for no inquiries into your condition will be made. In addition, each man will be directly responsible for the man in front of him in the column. You may not pass the man in front without first dispatching him. No ammunition will be used. When you mount the parapet, machine guns will be trained on you. Your only chance of life will be to go ahead.

When you meet the enemy, expect no quarter and show none. Unless he surrenders in large numbers and without a show of resistance, dispatch all prisoners. This applies also to the wounded.

Remember that the individual life counts for nothing. You are not considered as men, but as pennies in a game of give and take. There will be no retreat; if the enemy advances, he will do so only over your dead bodies.

Let's go!"

With that we made "squads right" and swung off into the all-enfolding night.

*   *   *

Oct. 3rd, Hospital, Langres

The lines -- the Hindenburg -- was 16 miles off, and we had to make the distance in six hours, to enable us to reform for the "zero hour." That, in itself, was enough as a preliminary for to-morrow's task, considering the load of ammunition we carried, but the road was taken up with horse and motor transport, which made the going extremely difficult. The rain of the pre-ceding day added its bit to the general unpleasantness, for if the roads were built of crushed stone there was enough clay to render them sticky and heavy. Under such conditions one's feet soon blister, and my case was no exception. But the real chafe was the degradation of being driven in a moving corral of bayonets.

We reached the objective on time with only three halts. Despite the cold night all were freely perspiring, but tired and hungry.

At one a.m. our guns broke loose in a perfectly wonderful tattoo. The thousands of field pieces and hundreds of larger guns, including naval rifles, belched forth as one. Every little bush and hollow had its battery, and the entire landscape behind us was one sea of fire. And noise...it was as if -- I thought -- as if the Almighty had in a moment of wild humor lent His whirlwinds and His thunder for an outing to a half-dozen fleas.

For the first four hours the larger number of shells were being expended on Jerry's wire and his first line of trenches. At this point No Man's Land was narrow -- only a couple of blocks -- so the shells had the emergency brakes on when they passed over us. A few fell uncomfortably short. But Jerry sure was getting merry hell.

The suspense of waiting was not easy to bear. The men were well nigh tuckered out by the long and furious march, having arrived perspiring to crouch for four hours of an intensely cold night in a colder trench. So all tried to busy themselves -- polish their rifles or adjust their harness. Others tried to hide their nervousness by recounting stories, from which all sentimentality was instinctively eliminated. To feel fear under the circumstances was natural; but to show it, or in any manner give way to it, was the sin unpardonable.

Many of these men were never to see another sunrise. Yet I dare say no thought went beyond the day's work. We were all fatalists -- for the day. Souls? If we had any, they had bally well to shift for themselves. There was more urgent business to hand.

For a moment I thought I saw a man in a prayerful attitude. And then and there welled up in me a furious hate of him. -- Trying to squeeze his puny, miserly soul into heaven, instead of taking his chances with the crowd! I felt a strong desire to kill him.

"Fix bayonets!" and in a moment we were Over the Top, in the shell-riven wilderness called No Man's Land.

As we climbed the parapet the first light of day was streaking the east. Making our way over the wire entanglements it occurred to me in a flash that this was my birthday. But my "wind" was not up -- then -- and I attached no importance to it.

Our shell barrage was just beginning to creep on, and our tanks were negotiating Jerry's wire.

I began to wonder what Jerry was doing. So far he had not replied to a single shell; his first line of trenches was entirely deserted. Our shells -- tens of thousands of them -- had gone for practically nothing. With the first shell he had 'pulled out', bag and baggage. Machine guns, the ideal weapon in defence, were left to deal with the attacking infantry. I later learned that what infantry he had he had sent to the rear.

For nearly two hours we crept at a leisurely gait behind the barrage, chatting and smoking and having a good time generally. For all we knew, Jerry was at home on leave with his frau and kindes. We were mistaken. He was merely lying low and biding his time. It came.

The larger number of our guns were "seventy-fives" (3 inch field guns). The effective range of these is little over five kilometres -- approximately three miles. By nine o'clock our barrage had practically suspended, the artillery moving up.

This is what Jerry had been waiting for. Ten minutes after his first shell came over, there was behind us a line of bursting shells. Simultaneously his machine guns began popping in front. We were in the open, with the supporting waves of infantry cut off. Then it was I decided Jerry was still on the job.

To make matters worse, our own artillery began replying -- with more vigor than prudence for many shells fell short, and a number of our men were killed. First Sergt. Kelsey was the first to go in Co. E -- I had never liked war. I liked it less than ever now.

To go ahead in an attempt to gather in the machine guns was impossible on account of our own artillery barrage. The major, who was with us, therefore gave orders to dig "foxholes." He himself was the only man to remain upright in an attempt to signal our planes and thus get the word to the artillery. He

received a bullet through the palm of his hand, but paid no attention to it further than to wrap his handkerchief around it. He was
a soldier and a gentleman, and the men would have followed him
through hell.

*   *   *

Undated

Our barrage soon lifted and we were able to proceed. This
was uphill work, though, for the resistance was stiffening meas-
urably. A few machine guns were being gathered in by our
scouts and tanks, but most of them just fell back alternately, one
gun covering the retreat of the other until it was ready to
resume fire and cover the retreat of the first. In this way, while
the enemy lost ground, he was enabled to get a dozen or two
men for one. He's a shrewd and keen fighter.

I regret that I cannot speak as well of our own command, for
if the men behaved in an exemplary manner, there was much
confusion, lack of co-ordination, and bad liaison. The line was
jagged with sharp salients, and the enemy therefore was continually getting in his murderous enfilading fire. But there was
enough excitement to go around and prevent introspection.
War is exceedingly stupid business.

The regiment was to proceed along the river Aire on the
right bank, and Co. E was on the extreme left, or next to the
river. At one point, opposite the town of Varennes on the left
bank, the bank was very high and steep. Here we were halted
and advised to "take cover" in shell holes (which were plentiful)
and wait until the first wave on the left was on a line with us.

To the north of the town, a half-kilometre or so, a belt of
trees stood out in line from the river. In this belt the enemy had
massed machine guns in readiness for the advancing infantry.
His artillery was by this time also in full play and the troops on
the left river bank marching on Varennes were suffering terribly.
The open which had to be crossed in the face of this fire I

judged to be about a mile square. Why our command elected to take the wooded belt by a frontal, massed attack without support of artillery seemed strange to me then (and it does yet), when it could be approached from the woods on the left which was already held by our men. But probably there were reasons a-plenty.

During the half-hour I crouched in a shell-hole on the promontory overlooking Varennes and the clearing to the west, my soul sickened with the spectacle of wholesale slaughter. Not content with the raking machine gun fire from the woods, the enemy was throwing shells with accuracy that suggested point blank range. Again and again the line was decimated, until the ground seemed mossgrown with khaki-clad bodies; but the support, spread out thinly, filled the gaps promptly, and the line moved steadily on.

When the line neared the woods the machine gun fire ceased as if at a signal, and doubtless the crews moved back. The fury of the German artillery was then turned on Varennes, and in the course of some thirty minutes it was reduced to little more than a pile of brick and mortar, battered out of all semblance. This senseless waste was evidently part of the German program, that nothing yielded up should be of worth, that France might be crippled the more in reclaiming. There is comfort in the thought that now, as I write, German prisoners are clearing the debris, the while paid by the German people. If that isn't justice, as well as vengeance, I miss in the fatalist way the meaning of the words.

* * *

(Entered in hospital at Chateauroux)

Oct. 5th

About 2 o'clock in the afternoon of the 26th the line halted at a road, the ditches affording excellent cover. What occasioned

The Wild Rose
Vol. 1   Headquarters 168" Inf. Between
No 11   A.E.F. FRANCE.   raids
                              May 22
                              1918

"AW SHUCKS,!
FRITZIE, YOU'LL
HAVE TO
AIM
BETTER'N
THAT!"

Walter
M.G. Co.

MOTHER

She is not young now and since
you came to France, a great anxiety tugs at her heart. She thinks
of you every waking hour, and at
night she seeks you in her dreams.
She is the best pal, the staunchest
buddy, the truest shipmate you ever
had. She never turned you down nor
quit you in a pinch, or left you
in the lurch. Your friend may desert you, your sweet heart may jilt
you. Your father may only be just
and kind, but your mother would die
for you. At this moment ther e is
an ache in her heart, a great hunger in her eyes and her entire being reaches out to you with a love
past understanding. Did you
write to her?

"G" Company.

A move farther from "Broadway"
means nearer Berlin.

COMPANY "E"

The Chaplain's effort to
supply us with things we like to
eat is appreciated the only
trouble seems to be that not
enough can be bought to supply
the demand but this is true of us
all for we have been so used to
getting anything in the States
that our little heart desires. In
France it is different.

MOTHER'S DAY was a big day
for all of us, and we are anxious
to know how fast the boats can
travel sending this message of
cheer and hope to waiting mothers.

Jim: (To boy reading his shirt)
      "Picking them out".
Sam: "No, just taking them as
      they come".

MAKE 168 INF. famous for its splendid, dashing, fighting qualities.

32

Pag e 2. WILD ROSE.

France, July, '18

Date ????

```
*****************************
*   The Wild Rose.          *
*Published by Chaplain W.E.Robb.*
*Herbert W. Freutel )Associate *
*Chester R. Hartzell) Editors  *
*****************************
```

MEMORIAL DAY.

The most impressive Memorial Day Service that it has ever been the w riters privilege to attend, occured at this Village May 30th, 1918. The sun was just sinking to rest as we gathered in the little French cemetery t o honor our dead. French and American soldiers f ormed a square around t he plot where our American soldiers sleep in Sunny France. Standing thus with bared heads the following program was given:

March -"Grandiso"---- Band,
"Songs of the Nation" Band
Reading Orders-Maj.Brewer
Prayer-----------Chaplain
Cornet Solo---Sgt.Morgan
Decoration of Graves--by
Officers & Frenc h chil-
dr en.
Address ------- Gen. Brown.
Addres s-----Col.Bennet t.
Song------------------"America".
Salute to the dead.
"Taps"--- Musician Bot ts
Benediction------Chaplain
March-"Amer. Life"--- Band.

ELIMINATE WASTE.

The folk at home are saving meat, wheat, money, time and labor. They are buying thrift stamps, Liberty Bonds, and giving money to the "Y" and the Red Cros s to Win The War.

Did you ever think every shell you waste delays the winning of the war. Every Gas Mask, every Helmet thrown away means some ones labor, money and sacrifices made in vain. ELIMINATE THE WASTE men, take care of your clothes, shoes, ammunition and equipment. ELIMINATE THE WASTE, fellows so we can win this durned old war and go home.

* * * *

A number of our men are wearing souvenirs imported from Germany direct via "Grenade Route". More are expected soon.

THE OUTPOST.

Dark nights, Black as pitch,
Eyes strained out thru the wire
Where death lurks in hole or ditch,
What's that? Gunner, Fire!

Red spurts stab the night,
A muttered oath, a groaning curse
A star shell cracks, and gleaming
    white.
I saw his face he was my first.

Weak and afraid, I stood and saw,
The drooping head, the limp dark
    form
Blood dripping from the shattered
    jaw,
The mud upon his uniform.

'Tis queer the tricks that darkness plays
Upon the nerves too tightly strung,
The morning sun's first slanting
    rays
Bade me rest, for I'd been stung.

Out in the tangled, torn u p wire,
The silent form that came to view,
Was naught to set my nerves afire,
A shattered stump, all scarred anew.

ENEMY BEATEN OFF IN ATTACK ON AMERICANS.

Heavy gas shelling precedes rush.

Amer.Front, Wednesday(delayed)
The Germans in the Luneville Sector, at half past twelve this morning, launched a heavy gas attack, then came over. The returned, or some of them did, and from the treatment they received in the hand to hand fighting it is likely they will wait some time before sailing into this particular group of Americans again.

About fifty Germans came over after the Gas Attack. They were met by some of the troops who went through the attack of the other nig t and bayonets and hand grenad. wer e used. Fourteen Germans go in the American trenches at one point. None returned. Ni ne were killed, and four are alive with wounds which are very serious. One died soon after being captured.

In this attack the Amer. casualities were very sm all. The Amer. soldiers in this section of the line are particularily bitter against the Prussians for thei r this halt I do not know, except it be that our flanks were "in the air."

Jerry was spending a lot of shells on our back areas, while the first line got off comparatively easy. However, one of his shells struck in the road and wounded a man of my squad in the leg, severing an artery, and our R.C. man could only partly check the blood. The major, who was with us, detailed two of us to carry the man to the first aid station which he said had just moved up to a wooded knoll about a kilometre to the rear, stating that we would have ample time to return before the forward movement resumed.

My canteen being empty, I hailed this task, intending to make for the river and replenish my water.

Between the knoll and the road was an open stretch, very probably in view of an enemy battery, for we had no sooner entered the open than shells began falling, now before or behind and to either side. This was evidently royal sport with the Germans, for they have been known on many occasions to waste shells out of all proportions on one or two men caught in the open, hounding them to death with high explosives. -- It may be sport for the gunners, but I dare say few of the victims relished it, for shells are fearful things, and fully equal to putting "the fear of God" in the heart of the stoutest.

A limp man is unbelievably heavy and progress was slow, especially after we started a zig-zagging course after the fashion of ships in the "danger zone." But Jerry kept shooting for the fun of it -- his fun -- and came uncomfortably near getting results with some of his shells. I was twice hit by flying sod with enough force to knock me over, and on one occasion a fragment of shell struck my helmet. I was convinced that a battery was trained on us, but doubtless this was the work of a "77" gun crew at play. My "wind was up" in a way that I had never before known fear -- almost panicky. Would not go through a like experience for all the medals in the world.

The knoll reached, Jerry turned his attention to searching for

34

the aid station, with the result that only charred stumps of trees are left. Fortunately the major was wrong in his assumption about the location of the station, which was located a good distance beyond.

Emerging from the wood, we deposited the wounded man in a shell hole and "took cover." I crept under a cart -- wanted a roof of some sort in the worst way. The "show" over, I discovered with mingled feelings, that the cart was loaded with ammunition; not the safest place when shell fragments were flying. But a miss is as good as a mile, 'tis said. I shall never volunteer as a litter carrier.

The "show" over, we took the man -- who long since had lost consciousness -- to the dressing station. After slaking our thirst at the stream and refilling our canteens, my fellow opened his tin of bully beef and ate heartily. I had no heart -- or stomach -- for food, although I had eaten nothing since the previous night. The fact was (and I realized it) that my "wind was up." A terrible, paralyzing fear had gripped me -- not the fear of getting killed, for that did not appear to inspire terror -- a condition that verged on panic.

The prospect of returning to the road where the company lay in wait, of traversing again the slope in view of the enemy and possibly be again subjected to point blank shelling, was therefore not alluring. But there were only the two alternatives; of returning, or deserting in the face of the enemy. Only the former was thinkable; but to start out called for some very severe mental discipline. Jerry had probably decided either that our cuticle was too thick, or that he hadn't our number. At any rate none of his shells struck near, although some were droning overhead on their way to our back areas.

As we set out, one of our tanks -- a "whippet," or "baby" tank -- which had probably met with difficulties earlier in the day and was now making for the front, was lumbering up the hill. We resolved to give this a wide berth, well knowing that tanks drew fire.

When on a parallel with this tank something happened to it which was probably not on its index as part of the day's work. It ran upon a large mine and disappeared. If it has yet been found I have no doubt some doctor has passed on its case as "shell shock" and after an application of iodine and C.C. pills marked it "duty." But grave doubts assail me as to whether it will pull together again. And the crew.

I had read about mines, but not till then realized what noise and hubbub a paltry few hundred pounds of dynamite can do when they have the will. Mines are fearful things. I'd hate to have one go off under my feet.

We found the company crouching in the same position, and indeed, lay there for a considerable time after we regained it. There was little doing except on our flanks, and I understand we were awaiting word from liaison officers.

It has occurred to me as strange that during all the time I have been at the front, I have never seen a fight between planes. One rarely sees planes of both persuasions in the air at the same time. Saw one Jerry shot down by an "Archibald" (anti-aircraft shell), and one of our planes apparently ran into a passing shell. But apart from the "sausages" these are the only ones I have seen brought down.

At times our planes would be overhead in swarms. At other times Jerry had the field to himself. Such visitations were anything but welcome, for they generally preceded heavy shelling; and I have the profoundest respect for German shells. I have learned to "take cover" without being told whenever the peculiar and unmistakable drone of the German plane was heard.

Shortly after regaining the company a lone Jerry airman came over and soon located us. With that he swooped down to within a few hundred feet and opened fire with a machine gun. He circled around and around, sweeping the ground with a deadly stream of bullets.

Someone began the counter-fire with a pot-shot at him, and soon everybody within range was shooting. Doubtless there were thousands of rifles blazing at him, but without avail. This despite the fact that he was so low I could see his face. I was much relieved to see him go.

Wellington wished for Blucher or night. I prayed for the sun to stand still over Askalon -- where ever that is -- convinced I would get outpost duty, which didn't appeal to me at the time. Had the keeping of the Allied cause been in my hands, I should have concluded peace then and there.

This once my fears were groundless, and in due time we dug "funk holes" (holes about six by two feet and two deep) and rested. This afforded some protection from shells, but not from the rain. I lay in soak, with my nose sticking out of the water. But my thirst left me.

About 9 in the morning Collins and myself were dispatched with a message to the artillery commander. This time it was the Colonel himself who instructed us, who took the trouble to write in duplicate, a copy for each. We were then to walk at least 20 yards apart, that the same shell may not stop both.

Not expecting any encounters, we slung the rifles by straps on our backs, and sheathed bayonets. The rifle straps passed over one shoulder and under the other, making it most difficult to recover them for quick action.

Thus equipped we stumbled upon two Germans in a shell hole who promptly threw up their hands. But the vision of two Dutchmen suddenly rising before us in this manner jolted us appreciably and I, at least, recovered the shooting iron in record time. The fact that they were not belligerent at the time, un-armed, and most anxious to be taken prisoner, was only one phase of the matter. They were German, and our minds were filled with thoughts on Germans -- and we were only passing brave.

How these two had managed to hide, and with what intent, I do not know. Our orders were to "dispatch prisoners and waste no ammunition" and good soldiers obey orders. Both Collins and I are indifferently "good" soldiers, so we took only their personal belongings (which is against the rules of civilized warfare), and marched them back to the artillery. Each got a "Gott Mit Uns" belt, correspondence and knickknacks. The Dutch say we fight for souvenirs anyway. We also took the trouble to remove their trouser buttons, that their hands might be occupied in holding up their trousers on the way.

(Nov. 25th, 1919 -- I still wear the belt, while the original owner is probably wrestling with wire entanglements in Northern France.)

*   *   *

Undated

Shortly after regaining the company we were relieved, and were in immediate support of the first wave. This meant that we would get the lion's share of the shelling but less of the direct machine gun fire. The big consolation was that the night would be less of a nightmare, as the first line would bear the brunt of counter attacks, if any, and there would be no outpost duty.

Being a "private in the army" when a genuine "show" is on is no cinch, all armchair singers of the Glory of War to the contrary notwithstanding. The lot of the average is bad enough, but if your stars are unfavorable, or if you have been refractory and are due for special castigation in the form of "detail" or fatigue, then may God have mercy on your soul.

Probably Collins and I deserved it -- deserved it mainly for not being smart enough to "get away with it" whenever we countered the rules. Anyway, we were reaping the rewards of ancient errors in a fashion well calculated to break the hearts and spirits, as well as the backs, of the stoutest. We were turned over to the M.C., given a litter between us and told to help gather in the wounded. Besides being hard work it was among the most dangerous, while we both decided it had but one redeeming feature, viz., of passing up wounded non-coms or officers for wounded buck privates. I was hoping we would find Lieut. R.

minus a leg or two sharing a hole with a buck. We would then leave him to the mercy of shells and carefully, lovingly lift the buck and convey him to the tender doctors. Collins hoped it would be the Colonel, saying while we were about it we might as well wish for a million as one dollar. Collins always was ambitious. We had no luck.

That afternoon we carried seven million (Collins kept count) men off the field, every last one of them weighing a ton up. (But we had our reward that night and will tell you all about it next week.)

*   *   *

Undated

When night fell Collins suggested that we fall back to some palatial dug outs we had passed earlier in the day and get what comfort we could. I don't know just what was expected of us, or how far into the night other stretcher teams worked, we were, in the words of Captain Katzenjammer, "at the end of the limit." For fifty hours we had eaten little and slept less -- slept not at all, in fact -- and much of this time we had been pitched to a high key of nervous tensions. There were oodles of mangled men on the field and other very valid reasons for staying on the job, but it couldn't be done; our sands had run out.

The dugout was a masterpiece of the "excavator's art," apparently fashioned for, and occupied by, high officers. There were no less than five rooms, quite well furnished, and bristling with souvenirs. In particular my fancy was caught by a spiked helmet of light tin surmounted by patent leather. If not quite a joy forever, it certainly was a thing of beauty! -- the kind they had on sale at Chaumont at "cent francs."

But what was of even greater moment was the fact that the kitchen was laden with good, nourishing food, with real cow's milk in the bargain. Was it a thousand times poisoned; was it deliberately left for our moppers? No matter, we were hungry

and ate with relish. Delicious bread made of (we have repeat-
edly been told) the bark of trees mixed with potato peelings;
honey cakes of maple sugar and other toothsome things; and
milk! After that we had a dozen or two of the Turkish cigarettes, thoughtfully left behind by the host. Only one disturbing
thought: the vulnerable side of the dugout turned towards the
enemy's guns, and he might conclude that some of our big fish
had taken shelter or possibly established a P.C. or dressing station in his erstwhile home. We decided to risk it, and slept the
sleep of the innocent.

Another hearty meal at sunrise and we set out with our litter
for the scene of action.

Where the Labourer who, upon faring forth in the morning,
never has felt at his heart a sinking sensation as of utter weari-
ness -- a dread of the day's toil well-nigh unbearable, when only
his sense of duty spurs him on? Refreshed as we felt after our
night in the dugout and the Jerry grub, neither Collins nor I
were much elated over the day's prospects. Not only was the
work heavy, but there probably -- very probably -- would be
shells to duck, and shells are most annoying.

But we had slept soundly during the night for we came upon
a gaping shell-hole in the path to the dugout entrance less than
a hundred feet off, that had not been there when we entered,
neither of us had noticed the explosion.

One consolation -- we worked independently. All we had to
do (and faith! 'twas enough) was to find the more severely
wounded, carry them to the dressing station, and return for
more. Collins insisted that the 35th was "all shot to hell" but
doubtless that was exaggerated. We didn't carry that many.

A new dressing station had been established in a dry creek-
bed, with a man-high perpendicular bank to the enemy. In this
respect it was safe from m.g. fire, but too wide to afford good
shelter from shell-fire, for as a rule shells fall at a steep angle.
We found this out shortly after noon (not after dinner, for we
had no dinner).

We had been carrying in the wounded all morning before the Germans turned their attention to the station. Doubtless they had seen where the wounded were being taken, and knowing distances and the lay of the land, "registered" their guns on the spot. They registered correctly, too.

Stray shells had been falling during the morning in the open from which the stretcher teams were trying to evacuate the wounded. Some of the wounded were no doubt placed further "hors de combat." One who had beckoned us helped to stop one of those shells. We had swerved to pick him up but the shell got there first. Most annoying, for we had to go further a-field to find another casualty.

We had just brought in a man when the first shell fell -- the first of the shells obviously meant for the station -- beyond, and a little to the left of, the station. The second fell just short. The third fell midway between the first two. It was typical German efficiency; and they always had a penchant for hospitals and dressing stations.

What took place during the next twenty minutes was terrible beyond attempt at description. Some 50-75 helpless men were lying about at the time, and many of these were killed or further mutilated. One of the two doctors was wounded, which left only five able-bodied -- the doctor, two M.C. sergeants, Collins and myself -- to move the wounded closer to the wall. This called for quick action, for the shells were wreaking fearful havoc, and did not allow of careful handling. The result was that men with all manner of wounds -- hands or feet torn partly off, with chest or abdominal wounds and others with faces horribly mangled piled indiscriminately against the bank.

When the barrage lifted we smoothed out the tangle as best we could, but these poor fellows were in for some further suffering, for gas started settling into the ravine. Those who could not abide masks on account of wounds were evacuated as soon as possible...

But all that is just war.

* * *

(Maison de Santé, Chateauroux, Department de Loire)

Oct. 10th, 1918. Abed.

During those two days Collins and myself acted as stretcher bearers, I kept wondering what the 35th N. G. was doing besides getting itself killed or wounded. It annoyed us how expert the men were at getting in the way of shells, and invariably coming out of the encounter second best. Collins was for taking a sentimental view of it, sometimes, but I couldn't follow him. -- Death, whatsoever whimsical and grotesque form it took, had ceased to affect me.

Once in a while we came upon fieldgray corpses -- but all too seldom. At a rough guess, I should say there were a hundred khaki to one field gray. One instance, however, heartened us, where a shell had lighted in a party of Germans and no less than fourteen of them were lying about. It did our tired hearts a world of good.

After a while we were hungered, and Collins was the first to give voice to it in the familiar and expressive "when do we eat?" Barkis was entirely willing, so we fell to after the necessary preliminaries -- said preliminaries being to find a corpse with reserve rations intact and a convenient shell-hole. Both were plentiful. We had long since thrown away our tins of bully beef and biscuit, bombs and the larger part of our ammunition, having other things to carry and proposing to live off the country.

It was nearing sundown, and we were straining under a load with Collins in the lead, when "my shell" came over -- the one with my name, serial number and home address. I had for some time been "listening in" on shells, but so far had failed to detect anything personal in their hiss.

This particular one fairly called my name, and from the first I knew it was the one. The burden fell and I crouched, turning half round to get behind the tin hat, as the proverbial straw to the drowning. I ceased breathing as the shell drew nearer, and when it finally started "putting on the brakes" my back humped and the feet were drawn in -- out of harms way. The picture is vivid to me after ten days because I have experienced it at least once every night. (Rewriting those blurred sheets after nearly fifteen months, the picture is still clear, from experiencing it times without number since.)

The impact shook us, and the ground rocked, but the explosion was not so terrific as I expected. There was a heavy thud, but the metallic fury of the high explosive was lacking...

I sat gasping, yet dazed, as if waking from some horrible nightmare. The muscles were tense, but not under control. I came fully to when Collins, speaking into his mask, called "gas" when I noticed that even the man on the litter had a mask on. The air had a strong sweetish flavor, not unpleasant. It broke upon me, with a shock, that we had encountered a gas shell. I got the respirator in place with all dispatch, but too late, for already the stomach was retching and soon my recent dinner of bully beef filled the facepiece. By the time I got back to the station my throat was dry and the eyes smarted. Every passing minute left me more sick and exhausted. My usefulness as far as this engagement was concerned was over.

-- Private. B. 2560815

* * *

Pvt. H.F. Bjarnason
Co. E. 139th Inf.
A.E.F.   Nov. 11th, 1918

Dear Inga:

Your letter intimating father's death came in today; also a letter from Triggvi of the 7th. Was glad to hear that he passed away quietly and without anticipating the end. I shall miss him very much when I come back, and the old homestead will never be the same, for besides being my father he was the man I respected the most, first, for his rugged honesty, and for his profound

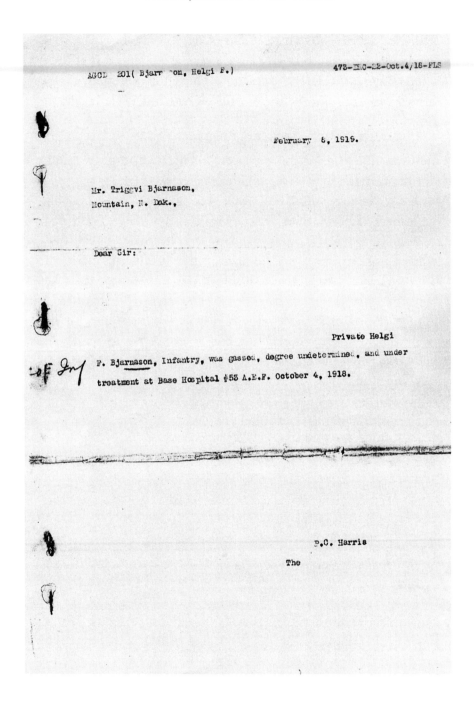

AGCL 201(Bjarr on, Helgi F.)   473-IRC-22-Oct.4/18-FLS

February 8, 1919.

Mr. Triggvi Bjarnason,
Mountain, N. Dak.,

Dear Sir:

                                                    Private Helgi

F. Bjarnason, Infantry, was gassed, degree undetermined, and under

treatment at Base Hospital #53 A.E.F. October 4, 1918.

                                        P.C. Harris
                          The

<u>education</u>. This may come as a surprise to you, but he was one of the few really learned men I have met.

But I have seen too much of death in its most terrible forms to be shocked any more; and keenly as I feel the loss, the battle-field aspect of death which I have acquired takes out the sting. But were mother to die before I got home I think I could never forgive her. It won't be so very long now to wait. All the <u>civilized</u> world tonight is rejoicing over the final victory. As I write, France is shouting herself hoarse.

My love and a kiss for mother. Probably I shall spend Christmas with you.

Bogi

*   *   *

This chapter concludes the series, the remainder dealing with ships and shoes and cabbages, and other things and matters not serving the purpose for which these fragments are published -- keeping the sordid side of war uppermost.

For war is sordid, cruel, and infinitely stupid. There is "glory" about a fresh regiment marching to music, but it soon dissolves into thin air on the field. The glorifiers of war will be found to be of the armchair variety, and should not be taken without discount; although time has a mellowing influence, and even those who have seen war at close quarters are apt to remember only the pleasant part and forget the disagreeable.

Don remembers overhearing stories told by three old "sweats," Dr. Lamont (Canadian Navy), Dad, and Ted Kane (Canadian Army). Mother was scandalized by the stories but, of course, a teenager would be fascinated and he would listen whenever and however he could.

One of the stories Don heard was a different version of the prisoners and the belt that Dad supposedly took from one of them. The Americans had a rest camp near the Alps not too far distant from a

German rest camp. As the only source of water was a small river running between the two, the two armies came into daily contact and they would exchange things from home and souvenirs, such as belts, etc. As this would not wash very well with the folks at home he created the bit about the two prisoners. But as he did not glamourize his part in the capture we can easily forgive his white lie. As the war wound down the people who were in danger of getting killed took precautionary measures, such as informing one another about barrages, etc., again, not mentioned. The "Gott Mit Uns" belt is now in the possession of, and is used by, Bogi's grandson, Peter Smith Bjarnason.

He also brought back the spiked helmet found in the dugout but left it behind in the Treherne Times office when we moved to Vancouver. When I returned to Treherne in 1981, Gary Lodwick, the present publisher and son of Al Lodwick who purchased the paper from Dad, professed no knowledge of it.

GLOSSARY

emma gees	-	*machine guns*
Dutchman	-	*a corruption of Deutsch (German)*
ack emma, pip emma	-	*am, pm*
go West	-	*to die*
Boche	-	*German*
Squarehead	-	*German*
cooties	-	*body lice*
buck	-	*buck private*
Captain Katzenjammer	-	*pompous comic strip character of the time*
sausages	-	*balloons*

Honorable Discharge from The United States Army

STATE OF NORTH DAKOTA,
ADJUTANT GENERAL'S OFFICE,
BISMARCK,
PAID IN FULL. $2.50⁰⁰

NOV 17 1924

UNDER THE PROVISIONS OF CHAPTER
206, SESSION LAWS OF 1919, AS
AMENDED. G. A. FRASER,
ADJUTANT GENERAL

TO ALL WHOM IT MAY CONCERN:

This is to Certify, That Helgi F. Bjarnason

2060815 Private, Co. E 139th Inf. (Co. D. Convalescent Center)

THE UNITED STATES ARMY, *as a* TESTIMONIAL OF HONEST AND FAITHFUL

SERVICE, *is hereby* HONORABLY DISCHARGED *from the military service of the* United States *by reason of* Telegraphic Instruction A. S. R. Nov. 15' 1918 and W. D. letter Nov. 30' 1918

Said Helgi F. Bjarnason *was born in* Mountain, *in the State of* North Dakota *When enlisted he was* 29 *years of age and by occupation a* Journalist *He had* Gray *eyes,* Brown *hair,* Light *complexion, and was* 5 *feet* 8 *inches in height.*

Given under my hand at Camp Dodge, Iowa *this* 21st *day of* June, *one thousand nine hundred and* nineteen

Emil H. Finke

Major Inf. U.S.A.

Commanding.

Washington, D. C. APR 12 1919
Paid $60 under Act of Congress, approved February 24th, 1919,
C. E. GRAY
Major, Q.

APR 17 1920
Paid add'l of travel pay under Act of Congress

Form No. 525, A. G. O.
Oct. 9-18.

* Insert name, Christian name first; e. g., "John Doe."
† Insert Army serial number, grade, company and regiment or arm or corps or department; e. g., "1,820,302"; "Corporal, Company A, 1st Infantry"; "Sergeant, Quartermaster Corps"; "Sergeant, First Class, Medical Department."
‡ If discharged prior to expiration of service, give number, date, and source of order or full description of authority therefor.

ENLISTMENT RECORD.

Name: *Helgi F. Bjarnason*   Grade: *Private*

~~Enlisted~~, or Inducted, *March, 29*, 1918, at *Cavalier No. Dakota*

Serving in *First*   enlistment period at date of discharge.

Prior service: * *— none —*

Noncommissioned officer: *No*

Marksmanship, gunner qualification or rating: † *— none —*

Horsemanship: *— Not mounted —*

Battles, engagements, skirmishes, expeditions: *Metzeral Aug. 28, 1918*
Argonne Forest Sept. 26, 1918

Knowledge of any vocation: *Journalist —*

Wounds received in service: *Gas — Lungs and heart —*

Physical condition when discharged: *— Good —*

Typhoid prophylaxis completed *April 20th 1918 —*

Paratyphoid prophylaxis completed *— April 20th 1918 —*

Married or single: *— Single —*

Character: *— Excellent —*

Remarks: *Service honest and faithful. No absence*
under AD 3/1912 and AD 45/1914. No AWOL.
non absence.

Signature of soldier: *Helgi F Bjarnason*

Ernest H Ruffels
2nd. Lt. Inf. U.S.A.
Commanding *Co. D. Con. B.*

*Give company and regiment or corps or department, with inclusive dates of service in each enlistment.
† Give date of qualification or rating and number, date, and source of order announcing same.

3—2164

48

CHAPTER 2

EDITORIALIST

Bogi Bjarnason was a newspaperman between 1915 and 1945. Over this period, he owned and operated several newspapers in rural Saskatchewan and Manitoba. He also worked in Winnipeg, briefly, publishing two Icelandic community newspapers. While he never worked for a large publication, Bogi was nonetheless well-known. John Bird, editor of the *Winnipeg Tribune* during the 1930s, called him "one of the province's most gifted newspapermen."

Bogi believed that a small town newspaper had several functions. Its most important function was to serve as a medium of self-expression for the town and its citizens. The newspaper also played an important role in facilitating local commerce and reporting news. Under no terms, however, did he allow his newspapers to be used for the narrow self-interests of individuals or organizations.

As a newspaperman, one of Bogi's primary tasks was writing editorials. His columns covered a wide variety of subjects, including economics, history, philosophy, and religion. When addressing politics, he commented on, and warned against, all sorts of domestic and international policies, from those that concerned the Depression to those that dealt with the looming conflict in Europe. No matter what the subject, his columns served to advocate the interests and concerns of rural Canadians and of Westerners. He also strived to both entertain and instruct his readers.

The following selection of editorials demonstrates Bogi's grasp of religion, politics, and history. They illustrate his capacity for using the past to predict the future. And they reveal his concern for the ordinary men and women, for whom he felt great compassion.

THE KELVINGTON RADIO

This is the editorial of the first edition of "The Kelvington Radio."
He named it that because of his interest in that new medium of com-
munication, the wireless radio. Bernice remembers their first radio as
having a pair of earphones. Don remembers it as having a large
horn speaker. The first issue is dated Nov. 30, 1922 and cost "5 cents
the copy; $2.00 the year."

"The Wayside Pulpit" was a boxed item which was placed imme-
diately above the editorial and on this day read: "The Lord Saith,
Let There Be Light. – The Light of Publicity is Incandescent, And
Pierceth the Darkness of Ignorance."

*   *   *

"TUNING IN"

THE KELVINGTON RADIO in its first broadcast goes
into practically every home in the district tributary to Kelvington,
confident that it will everywhere find a welcome and a reception
"tuned" to its "wavelengths." Into many of these homes it goes
unbidden, begging a crumb of attention. Where it meets with
approval it will expect consideration -- the usual subscription fee
-- and will then come again, growing, as we hope it will grow, in
vigor and interest with every passing week, bringing News of the
Neighbor and the neighbor's neighbor. Where not so welcome it
will expect clear intimation to that effect without delay, that the
mailing list may be altered accordingly.

The first number is being issued under difficulties, some of the material well-nigh indispensable to the mechanical production of a paper being still enroute. With more material to work with we hope to give it in the course of time a more finished appearance. The staff is new to these parts and therefore not in a position to know all about everything going on. That both of these shortcomings will be presently overcome admits of no doubt.

The aim is to make The Radio a live, well gotten up newspaper, carrying all the local news fit to print -- a newspaper to do justice to Kelvington and which may be a credit to town and district. It can, of course, only do this if loyally supported by subscriber and businessman.

The best news it can hope to bring to any subscriber will be the trade news -- the advertisements of local merchants, businessmen and professional men crying their wares or services. Its first and main service will be in bringing together buyer and seller to their mutual benefit. The subscriber will learn to read and profit from the advertising columns, just as the merchant will learn that advertising is Good Business, and is being done in all enlightened countries for the sole reason that it pays.

THE RADIO owes its inception to a local demand for a medium of local expression. It owes allegiance to no party or clique, is independent in politics, and reserves the right to comment on anything whatsoever, local or general. It reserves, further, the right to make its quota of mistakes, for it is now fairly well established that newspapers are not above falling into error. Its mission is to bruit abroad the fame of an excellent community, urban and rural; to record the daily living of Mr. and Mrs. Kelvington and family, to praise them when they do well, to chide them, mayhap, when naughty; to congratulate them on getting born, to marry them off "prettily," and inter them in black borders. It does not undertake to tell the whole truth and nothing but the truth at all times, for on occasion it makes for amity to slur over or stretch a point. Thus we might

Photo dated 1920s.

choose to say that God called Mr. Soandso when really he died in agony from sampling his own brew. But other things being equal, it will endeavor to tell of things as they happen, if they bear telling at all, and to comment fairly and impartially on things as they are and as it thinks they should be.

The editor is not entirely new at the game, having been in the business for seven years. (He is a veteran of the late European fracas, and is now somewhat handicapped in the pursuit of riches and happiness by reason of the insistence of a German shell in contesting that particular spot of northern France he stood on.) And in these seven years in the newspaper game he has learned a few things and unlearned not a few others. He can confidently boast of having taken one to heart -- not to speak unkindly of anyone, whatever the monetary provocation suggested. He has said many an unkind word in the past, not one of which has failed to come home to roost. The power of the printed word is great, and lasting. It is dangerous in proportion to its power, and particularly so in a restricted community, where everybody knows everybody else and personal feelings are easily aroused. He therefore begs to be excused from airing grievances, grinding axes or violently "taking sides" except in cases bearing on the public weal. Those who look for personal bickering and the insinuation so common with small town papers will look for it in vain in our columns.

These general principles understood, THE RADIO bids a cheery "bon jour" to all its well-wishers.

*   *   *

1923

The Bible, like figures, can be made to prove anything, either way, or to support anything, from monogamy to Bolshevism. The man who quotes the Bible in support of some pet contention could, in most cases, also quote it to prove the exact opposite.

Thus the following, which we came across in 1st Timothy, 5-23, can be used as anti-prohibition propaganda. "Listen! -- Drink no longer water, but use a little wine for thy stomach's sake, and thine often infirmities."

*   *   *

Farmer Brown was somewhat surprised, it may be assumed, when one of John D's oil tanks drove into his farmyard and asked him what he was paying for oil that day. Brown took one barrel at his own price, and John D's man drove away, apparently satisfied.

Farmer Brown was even more surprised when the Massey Harris man drove in with a binder to inquire what binders were fetching that day.

And that very day the mail brought him two parcels, one from T. Eaton and one from his bank. The first was a parcel of household necessities, which a polite letter accompanied, requesting him to "kindly favor us with remittance for package of merchandise this day shipped to you at prices current with you." The other was a bundle of bills to which was appended a letter requesting him to please forward us your note for enclosed at the interest rate you are now paying.

And one dunner the mail brought farmer Brown this self-same day -- from the doctor. "Dr. I. Curem, for officiating at birth of child. Your current rate for same."

In the cold grey dawn farmer Brown awoke. He had been dreaming. Such things as those recorded above do not happen in real life.

Yet when farmer Brown ships his can of cream, his crate of eggs or poultry, he requests the consignee to "remit at your current rate." When he hauls his wheat to the elevator he asks, "What are you paying for wheat today?"

Having disposed of his wheat at "your current price" he goes to the store to buy shoes or sugar. He is not asked what he is paying for shoes or sugar today. The price is fixed for him both ways. He "gets it coming and going." Quite often he gets it in the region of his windpipe.

Consider. Here is the greatest industry in this country, in this world for that matter, told, and emphatically told, just what prices it can receive for what it produces, and then told, still more emphatically, just what prices it must pay for the necessities it must have. It is dictated to when it sells and when it buys.

Like the circus elephant it performs and works for a master. The master is organized capital. Proportionately the farmer has infinitely more power than the elephant, but like the brute he is helpless before the keeper with the hook.

The elephant has the strength but lacks the intelligence. The farmer has the intelligence but lacks the organization. Neither is getting the full fruit of his labor.

*   *   *

The writer is being circularized by some church brotherhood in the U.S. to contribute towards a $100,000 fund to send missionaries to China. Wonder what that same brotherhood would say if an equivalent body of the Sons of Confucius contemplated such a drive against Christianity in America?

*   *   *

The Lord's Day Alliance of Canada have given notice that they will appeal the unanimous decision of the five appellate judges of Manitoba, making legal the operation of Sunday excursion trains from Winnipeg to Winnipeg Beach. These excursion trains enable working men and their families whose circumstances do not allow of automobiles to get away from the heat of the pavements one day a week, but the Alliance claims they should devote the day to church activities. Those who command automobiles are independent of trains and go anyway. The operation of trains would give the poorest families the same opportunity. This privilege the Alliance would deny them. -- It's a strange world, and a foolish one.

* * *

When we consider that thirteen hundred thousand earths, like our own, could be taken into the sun through one of the holes on its surface which we call "sun spots" and that the sun is but as a single grain of sand compared with the number of the heavenly bodies, we get a faint idea of the earth's littleness, and of the immensity of the universe. Yet man, an infinitesimal atom as compared to the earth, considers himself the centre of the universe. He has long had an exalted opinion of himself, and time isn't modifying that opinion very much.

* * *

The writer was taught in American schools to detest the name of Great Britain, to look upon England as the traditional enemy -- all in the name of history.

In Canadian schools the child is taught to look upon the United States as a questionable friend. Canadian history, as taught in Canadian schools, says the war of 1812 was a war of aggression against Canada on the part of the States, waged for conquest and spoils. American history says this war was a protest against the impressment of seamen into British service, against the practice of British men-of-war exercising the right of search of American merchantmen on the high seas.

The two opinions conflict. Both are not right. Quite likely both are wrong.

So it comes about that history is not history at all, but a series of mischievous half-truths, written with the intent of perpetuating animosities in the name of "patriotism." Instead of healing the hurts of war it seems to keep alive the hatreds and bequeaths to the young a legacy of ill will.

American history needs re-writing and re-teaching; Canadian

history also. History, as taught in the common schools the world over, is not guiltless of the late war.

There is enough strife and bitterness in the world without seeking to instill in the young mind the hatreds of the fathers, -- the residue of misunderstandings and mistakes of former generations.

* * *

This is a time of vacations. All those who are working, or think they do, are taking holidays and resting from their labors.

This is eminently fitting and necessary. It is most essential in the case of the employee who considers himself indispensable, and who has developed a degree of fatty degeneration of the ego. He learns how easily he is dispensed with, how easily his place can be filled. It is no less necessary for the employer who thinks he is carrying the weight of the world on his shoulders, and that the bottom will drop out of things if for a moment he relaxes his vigilance. A few days absence will tell him that he, too, is not quite indispensable.

Outside of this vacation serves no useful purpose.

Being rather "close with a dollar," vacations and travel were rather low on my father's list of priorities.

* * *

Sir Edmund Walker, sometimes called the "Dean of Canadian Bankers," urges farmers to "work harder and do without some of the comforts of life they now enjoy." Roll your own comment on that.

1924

Who discovered America? (Not that it matters.) Ask one

hundred average men and ninety and nine of them will answer quickly and emphatically, "Christopher Columbus." This despite the fact that school histories and encyclopedias assert that the discovery of the western hemisphere by Europeans was made five hundred years before Columbus; and that Columbus never saw the continent. (This Columbus legend was recently pressed upon us so hotly that we were forced to study the subject. Hence this outburst.)

The first white man whose eyes beheld any part of the American continent was the Icelander, Bjarne Herjulfson, in the year 968. The first white man who, to our certain knowledge, planted his feet upon American soil, was Lief Eriksson (also an Icelander, as were all those who followed, prior to Columbus), in the year 1000. The first white man to be buried beneath American soil was Lief Eriksson's brother, Thorvald, in the year 1002. The first white man who founded a settlement in America was Thorfinn Karlsefni, in the year 1007. The first white woman who came to America was Thorfinn's wife, Gudrid. In the year 1008 she gave birth to a son in Vinland. The boy was named Snorri, and he was the first person of European descent to see the light of day in the new world.

With these facts indubitably established it is remarkable how the Columbus myth persists in the popular mind. Prior to his day books had been written about the land to the west, and its location was known. Columbus knew about it, and made a voyage to Iceland to learn all he could. His first great feat was to overcome the opposition of the church, which maintained that the earth was flat, and his introduction of pelagic navigation. Prior to his first voyage all nautical knowledge was limited to coast navigation, if the pagan Norse Vikings are excepted. Not hampered by southern superstition, which peopled the unknown with terrors and stifled all progress, they had then for centuries sailed the high seas at will.

*   *   *

Struggling with the catechism in days long gone, we were impressed with the force and number of "Thou shalt nots." And the command never failed to suggest that the thing or act thus condemned was something sweet and desirable. In this respect the years have not changed us very much.

*   *   *

Things we'd Like to Know: What is the voltage of the Christianity generated by the friction of two or more Women's societies in a small town?

1925

Just now we are wondering whether it is a good sign or a bad that our observations under this head almost invariably "back-fire." Whether the subject be kings or cabbages, ships or sealing wax, some reader is certain to find in our treatment of it something not squaring with his own ideas. If he doesn't like it he tells us, if the occasion presents itself; if anyone has ever agreed with anything that has appeared here we have yet to hear of it. But that is not to be wondered at.

A day or two ago a reader took us to task -- by the scruff, figuratively speaking -- and laid the lash of his tongue to our back so vigorously that we felt like Quasimodo on the turnstile. And all because we had had the temerity to say that the church, and what we call Christianity, could be trusted to oppose the new Danish penal measure -- a measure so far in advance of the times that its practicability is doubted, until public opinion can catch up with it. The church is by its very nature conservative and intent on holding onto things long overdue in limbo. It is the "Defender of the Faith" first, last and all the time. Faiths change, as all things change, but the church is the last to take note of it, and so is always too late, bringing up the rear instead of leading in the march of progress. It is changing, as it must, accepting the new when it can no longer ignore it, but rarely with good grace. It has held up pious hands in horror at every "new-fangled" idea down the ages, ready to crucify or burn any or all of the intrepid and independent thinkers. The Son of Nazareth was so far in advance of the times that some of his teachings are only now beginning to seep in, and then find favor first with Chicago lawyers and Danish statesmen. His "But I say unto you" has been treated by the church as merely a goody-goody Sunday school platitude, beautiful as an ideal but impossible in practice. So far as we know the Mosaic penal law is in effect throughout the civilized world, and has the solemn "amen" of the church. This is why we referred to it in these columns as "so-called" Christianity.

*   *   *

Some three hundred years ago an obscure cabinet maker in a small Italian town took to making violins. As time went on he altered the form of the instrument, as known then, bringing it to the shape and size as we know it today. From that day to this every conceivable thing has been tried to improve on the methods of Stradivarius, but in vain. Its fifty-seven component parts, as arranged by the Violin-maker of Cremona, three hundred years ago, defy all attempts at rearrangement or alteration, and his instruments remain the dream of violinists and the despair of violin-makers.

And what a wonderful thing is that violin. While in every branch of human knowledge and activity every year marks new discoveries, and the apparent miracle of today becomes the common thing tomorrow, the violin stands where it stood three hundred years ago, and every attempt at altering its form or any smallest part of it has been a dismal failure. Is it not as if for once human wit has reached its goal, as if the ideal hid in the heart of God has for once been grasped by man?

*   *   *

Colonel Webb, mayor of Winnipeg, in a recent speech at Yorkton, deplored the talk of secession of the west from the east. In another speech of a later date, he suggested that the western part of Ontario might profitably secede and join the province of Manitoba. This on the ground that the western rim of Ontario was so placed geographically that it was more easily administered from Winnipeg than from Toronto, and that it had problems in common with Manitoba and less with the rest of Ontario.

The Colonel, with all due respect be it said, is not very consistent in this. The problems of eastern and western Canada are vastly farther apart than the problems of eastern and western Ontario. Canada has always had, and will have, so far ahead as anyone can see, a government from east of the Ottawa River. While not strictly inimical to the west, Montreal capitalists cannot reasonably be expected to have the understanding of western problems necessary to further its best interests. The eastern viewpoint is that of industries and capital; the western viewpoint is agricultural. There is a vast hiatus between the two, too great to bridge by any artificial means. It may be said that the two viewpoints are diametrically opposed. The east, having the whip hand, is going ahead with the minimum of consideration for western problems, and is widening the gap at every step. Where that policy will lead is still in the sleeve of time.

Worthy mayors and other leading men may "deplore" with all their might, but so long as the east remains in the position of being able to call the tune and dance, and the west pays the piper, there will be talk of secession. Much of it may be talk and talk only. A good deal of it is foolish and idle talk. Nevertheless it is symptomatic of a condition which requires something more than "deploring."

Treatment -- fair treatment -- and some inkling of sympathetic consideration from the east is needed. It is all that the west demands.

*   *   *

Hon. Mr. Lynch-Staunton: "What do they do in the House of Commons? I have before me the second volume of Hansard, 3000 pages of talk, which has gone on there since the opening of parliament, and if there was one idea that was not known before, or one argument that has not been made a hundred times in these 3000 pages, I will eat it."

Right Hon. Sir George E. Foster: "You would have much wind on the stomach."

(Extract from Senate Debates.)

*   *   *

Talk to us, Mr. King. We can stand a lot of that kind of punishment. But spare, oh! spare us your promises.

*   *   *

Every week there come to this table a score or more of "exchanges," weekly local papers published in the area bounded by Nipawin on the north, Naicam on the west, Wynyard-Yorkton on the south and Kamsack-Swan River on the east. Each one is scanned for what meat, in the way of news or ideas, it may have. As a general rule, the search is fruitless. If we except the Yorkton Enterprise, which is ably edited, the lot of them is a vapid and colorless lot, and about as interesting as mediocrity can make them. Much of what news they carry is poorly presented, and the whole an unedifying hodge-podge of boarding-house leftovers, without the condiments. Whether the Radio is on this order is not for us to say, lacking the perspective necessary for detached judgement.

We are moved to the use of strong language by reading, every now and then, about some man in one high public position or another extol the large and beneficial influence of the local press. That such remarks are, as a general rule, post prandial, when compliments are decidedly in order, may have something to do with it.

That the local press is what it is cannot be wondered at. Few of those who drift into the trade are fitted by education, training or natural ability for journalism -- the task of keeping the public informed of its own doings, and the running alongside of marching events to point out their significance. A great many of those engaged in the small town weekly field have begun as chore boys in printshops and, through sheer lack of initiative, have stayed with it until they "went into business for themselves" and found themselves "publishing a newspaper." Much of the attendant work is drudgery, uninspiring and unremunerative. Result -- the ordinary local paper.

What place or purpose these papers have in the general scheme of things is less clear to us the larger number of them we see. We feel safe in saying that if ninety-five percent of them were to suspend not a ripple would result -- they would settle into the grey gloom of oblivion and be promptly forgotten, as they deserve to be. Whether they are merely the reflection of the minds of the class of people they presume to serve is another matter, and one on which we do not care to register an opinion.

This may have been occasioned by the item below. He was always very careful about the use of the English language and was very critical of misuse of it by anyone who he felt should know better.

Replying to an item in a recent Radio on the currency question, the "Herald," of Wadena, said, in part (the words quoted being reproduced here exactly as they appeared in the "Herald"): "Thus wheels move within wheels and commodity values, effected by trade conditions appear to be the real magnet. Sir Henry in his remarks mentioned wheat as very susceptible to rapid inflation or deflation because of its easy and rapid transportation and its short stage of manufacture. If inaugurated control and not be made the means of it should be subject to very careful undue inflation." -- That ought to settle the question. Indeed, if the currency-reform movement can stand treatment of this kind it is proof against any adverse winds that may blow.

*　　*　　*

My copy of this editorial does not have the masthead attached so I have no date for it. The only indication that I can offer for its time of printing is that the last editorial for which I have a positive date is Dec. 23, 1926. I never found out the reason why he gave up the newspaper.

"FADING SIGNALS"

One of the mysteries of radio broadcasting and receiving is the "fading signal." The receiver "picks up" a sending station. The broadcast comes in loud and clear. Then, for some reason not yet understood, the broadcast becomes fainter and fainter, finally dying out, or it may cease abruptly in the middle of a word. The phenomenon is known as the "fading signal." With static, it enjoys the reputation of being one of the two greatest obstacles to absolute success in radio broadcasting.

Something akin to this has no doubt been noted by listeners-in to station KR. The weekly programs have not been up to fond expectations, either as to quality or manner of presentation, for causes not necessary to set forth here.

Beginning next week however, the microphone in the sanc-tum will be in new, and probably abler, hands. So stand by, folks. -- KR now signing off. Good-bye. B. B., announcer.

TREHERNE TIMES

His first editorial, dated May 8, 1930.

In assuming control of *The Times* a decent respect for the opinions of its readers impels the new management to briefly set forth its beliefs, policies and aims to which it will in the future strive to adhere. A long journalistic career in the small-town field has tested these beliefs and found them not wanting. This, then, is the credo:

A firm belief in the workability of the Golden Rule in the every-day contacts of life.

A generous belief in the inherent decency and integrity of the Average Man in ordinary dealings, placing him above suspicion of motives.

A large belief in the future of Canada -- and particularly of Western Canada -- as a land worthy of the best that a man can give to its upbuilding, a land of which any man may own to with pride as his home.

A large belief in the Commonwealth of British Nations -- welded into a whole as The British Empire -- as an influence for good in the hegemony of peoples.

A warm belief in the old-fashioned home of family life, in public non-sectarian instruction, in the church as an influence for good, in a thorough respect for the law of the land, and in the old standards of private and public morals. (This may appear to be stating the obvious; but on not a few occasions of late we have found ourselves staring in bewilderment, wondering whether a new and strange world has come into being while our gaze was turned to a world that was, but is no more.)

These principles set forth, *The Times* renews its lease of life in the trust that it may retain old friends and gain new ones. It will at all times endeavor to record news of local interest fairly and impartially, to offer its opinions on matters of public interest when it feels competent to do so, and to direct whatever influence it may have to forward whatever is, according to its lights, in the general weal.

The Times (to forestall misunderstanding on this point) owes allegiance to no party, clique or sect and will not "sell out" or serve as trumpet for any particular body of opinion or interest. In politics it is neither Tory, Grit nor Progressive, holding that no one party is the sole keeper of the right on every issue, but reserves the right to praise or criticize where it believes such praise or criticism to be merited.

This understood, *The Times* extends a cheery "bon jour" to all its well-wishers.

Bogi Bjarnason

*   *   *

Following are editorials, excerpts from editorials, and various small items selected from his collection of writings in the "Treherne Times" from May, 1930 up to the spring of 1945. I have had to be arbitrary in my choices, but have tried to take representative samples that will give a feel for the times. It would be helpful if we do not forget that the economic and stock market bubble burst in a rather spectacular fashion on Oct. 29, 1929; "Black Tuesday." This set the stage for "The Great Depression," which was deep, long, and virtually worldwide, and which did not end until we were well into the Second World War. At that time, the social service network which is now in place in Canada did not exist and a person who found himself out of work was truly on his own. The last resort was "relief," which was dispensed in miserly amounts and a manner designed to deliver the maximum of embarrassment and humiliation along with the minimum of money.

He did not date his clippings when he inserted them in his scrapbooks, each of which contained two years of clippings. So the only positive date I have is at the beginning of most years. I have entered these whenever I've had them.

1930

The Average Citizen of Western Canada, scanning the newspaper at his ease after the evening meal, may with some reason pause in his reading to remark that things are not all right side up with care. He may well be excused for allowing this thought to intrude upon his rest while reading of breadlines numbering hundreds in such towns as Brandon and The Pas in early summer in Western Canada! And his thoughts are justified; there is something radically wrong, either with Western Canada of itself, or with the world at large, from which we suffer in sympathy. He may not presume to know what that something is, but it requires no seventh son to realize that whatever that condition is, it is "getting no better fast."

It may be argued that a variety of reasons contribute to bring about this condition. The six or eight years of a "bull market" came to a sudden and sharp termination last fall when forty billion dollars in stock values was written off in the United States and five billion in Canada; our comparatively small exportable surplus of high grade grain goes begging on the markets of the world: resultant lack of buying power curtails production, and unemployment ...

But whatever the reasons, we have with us in this year of grace 1930 formidable lines of able-bodied and willing workers at a time of year when such men should be at a premium in this most progressive country in the world. And the end is not yet ...

*   *   *

Hon. T. A. Crerar, Minister of Railways and Candidate in the Brandon constituency, said in a speech at Brandon last week that "there has never been a time in the whole history of the Dominion that this country has been so prosperous as now -- and this prosperity is due, in large measure, to the King government." -- So there's the explanation. Honestly now, we didn't know where all the prosperity we are enjoying originated.

*   *   *

A goodly portion of the world's economic and industrial problems, the unemployed millions and general depression is blamed on overproduction. Which leads Heywood Broun, the famous American journalist, to remark that when monkeys come into a period of over-production -- such as a glut of coconuts -- they have a picnic: But when men experience a glut they have a panic, followed by starvation and distress, for the only reason that they have too much. Well, it may be too much to ask of mere man -- homo sapiens -- to meet a problem of this nature with the same degree of good sense as a monkey. Maybe it's that. It certainly looks that way.

*   *   *

1931

During the year of grace (or is it disgrace?) 1930 the people of Canada drank $200,000,000 (two hundred million) worth of intoxicants. A special session of parliament was called last fall to enable the government to vote relief to the extent of $20,000,000 (twenty million), just one tenth as much, for the alleviation of distress. -- This is a funny world!

*   *   *

After the war of 1763 French and English plenipotentaries met to adjudicate peace. England held out for territory as the spoils of war, demanding the island of Guadeloupe. France offered Canada instead. England demurred on the ground that Canada was barren and practically valueless. Through the efforts of Benjamin Franklin England finally accepted Canada. And now not one of three readers of this can find Guadeloupe on the map without first looking it up in the index of an encyclopedia.

* * *

A dozen Australians and New Zealanders arrived at Vancouver recently, with the purpose of making their homes in Canada if that seemed feasible to them after a study of conditions. They were refused entry on the grounds that their efforts to make a living in this country might deprive some of those already here of necessary work, and were accordingly sent back. They were, however, first allowed one day's shore leave at Vancouver where they found "Prosperity Week" in full swing, and posters in the streets proclaiming: "The sun is rising on the greatest year of Canada's prosperity."

* * *

The two Canadian railway systems are said to be losing on operating expenses at the rate of a million dollars a week each, or well over one hundred million dollars annually. A half of this sum, that incurred by the National system, will eventually have to come out of government coffers and so is of more direct concern than that of the C.P.R., but the whole is assuming proportions that are thoroughly alarming. The plan which necessarily suggests itself is that the two systems should be combined to effect economies by cutting out unnecessary duplication, and no doubt large savings could be effected. Which one should swallow the other is another thing again.

*   *   *

One of the things that may well be a matter of concern to the average taxpayer in Canada is the rising cost of government. The breadwinner for an average family of five now contributes the earnings of one day in four to pay taxes, direct and indirect, a sum of $508.25 annually, federal, provincial and municipal. And this does not include C.N.R. deficits which he pays as well. Fifteen percent, one in seven, of the population of Canada, gain their living directly or indirectly from the government. More people work for the federal, provincial and municipal governments than work in all the 6000 factories in our twenty-two leading manufacturing industries. In 1912 the total annual taxes paid directly and indirectly by the average family was $165.00; in 1920 this had increased to $405 (due largely to the war); but in the last ten years this has increased by another $100. The government of Canada today collects more in one year in Toronto than it collected in all Canada in one year before the war. Small wonder that the cry for some consolidation of government services has arisen.

*   *   *

Violin music is produced by drawing the tail-hair of a dead horse across the entrails of a dead cat. The thoroughgoing cynic may, indeed, see in the instrument nothing beyond this fact, while the man who looks beyond the rim of things recognizes the voice of Beethoven in the friction of bow and strings. And much of life is like that. Things in and of themselves may be sordid, while the uses to which they are put may be noble if vision inspires the act.

*   *   *

It is doubtful if there ever was, since the dawn of moral consciousness in man, a generation of older people who did not lament the flightiness and lack of moral responsibilities of the younger generation. The earliest writings bear this out, each of the older generations in turn indulging in lugubrious head-shakes over the follies of its successors. When a man is yet young with much of life before him he is apt to take things with only a mild degree of seriousness; but let him turn down the homeward stretch of life, with waning strength and lessening powers of enjoyment and forth-with he begins to gaze over his shoulder, not so much at the capering youngsters on the first lap as at the reflection on his own youth. He sees the youngsters enjoying themselves with pleasures of which he can no longer partake, and the feeling that he himself did not fully enjoy his opportunities in this respect in his youth sours him and he be-grudges the youngsters the fun they are having and in which he can no longer share. That he is not aware of the underlying reasons for his deploring of the ways of the young goes without saying: but the root is there. As a foil against consciousness of the waning of his own powers of enjoyment he dons a cloak of heightened moral feelings and responsibilities. He condemns the sins and follies of his own youth and of those who are now following in his own footsteps for the only reason that he can no longer find enjoyment in them. "Twas ever thus." – There is a great deal more of truth than of poetry in the following quatrain:

> King Solomon and King David
> Led merry, merry lives,
> With many, many lady friends
> And many, many wives;
> But when old age came upon them
> With its many, many qualms,
> King Solomon wrote the Proverbs
> And King David wrote the Psalms.

*　　*　　*

[Item from The Chronicle, Cavalier, North Dakota]

THE SAME IN CANADA, TOO

Here's some comment published in the *Treherne* (Manitoba) *Times* as written by Bogi Bjarnason, publisher of the paper, a former resident of Pembina county, a scholar who watches with a keen eye and clear mind the progress of the world, poignantly points his logic at the centralization of wealth as being the sole cause of the present state of the economic world. You'll appreciate his views in the ensuing paragraphs, which are heartily in accord with those of the Chronicle. He says:

"Much is heard about the ring of Montreal and Toronto financiers who hold in their hands the economic and industrial reins of the country and are in position to determine our economic well-being. There is, unfortunately, a large percentage of truth in that statement. A dozen men, more or less, heads of the larger banks, power, paper, utility, insurance and holding companies control so much wealth that to name the aggregate is almost staggering. They are the real, if invisible government. Because directorates interlock, the group becomes a family with identical interests.

What they cannot do by group action is almost beyond the conceivable. What they do is plenty, if we can believe charges made public. Instances of large-scale rifling are bared, whereby the public is fleeced of savings for worthless stock and companies loaded with debts under which they cannot rise. All the time the individuals in the inside circle are getting richer and extending the holdings which they control, and the cost of it all is passed on to the consumer in increased prices and taxes, while at the same time the ability of the workman to meet them is lessened. How the corner to prosperity is to be turned in the face of such conditions is not explained, much as we hear about the imminence of this blessed event.

It may be that the nation will rise superior and work its way out of the maze, irrespective of what this massive concentration of capital does about it. It may be. But the odds do not wholly favor that happy solution. It may be also that politicians, seized of the danger of the situation will tinker with the works till it gets going. If it is sincere in the matter the federal government can do much to curb predatory financial activities and undo some of the mischief already wrought. But as quoted above, if the system goes down to ruin it will not be the doings of Tim Buck* and his ilk, but by reason of the depredations of the 'big shots' who are milking the cow white and haven't the sense to know when to call a halt.

We have in Canada the counterparts of the Rothschilds, Sassoons, Creusots, Zaharoffs and Thyssens of Europe and the Du Ponts, Mellons and Morgans of this country do just what those named have done to theirs. Which, to repeat, is PLENTY."

Mr. Bjarnason has the correct understanding of this situation. Despite our New Deal nothing seems to have been done in this country to any great extent to prevent the further centralization of wealth. Although we claim no relationship with prophecy, it is safe to assume conditions will remain acute until this huge financial octopus ceases to spread its tentacles to suck further the life blood of a great commonwealth. It remains the root cause of our dilemma.

*Tim Buck was the leader of the Communist Party of Canada.

* * *

1932

It may be stated with a high degree of assurance that few will regret the passing of 1931. It has been a fairly difficult year in more than one sense, throughout the entire world. Economic and political disaster have all but stalked western civilization, periodically threatening to overtake and engulf it. That this danger is by no means over cannot be gainsayed; but somehow the passing of a milestone seems to associate the danger with the past rather than the future. The great hope that this danger may be in large measure averted lies in the general recognition that it exists. Statesmen of the great powers are cognizant of the focal points of danger, and they are many. There is the further fact, for which all may give thanks, that none of the great powers want large scale war at this time. They may stumble into it, but not willingly.

What are the great dangers? Undoubtedly the greatest is that some of the first-class powers go down suddenly to economic chaos and internecine strife. Germany, for one, could very easily do this, and the repercussions in other countries of such a crack-up might be disastrous. There is India, seething on the verge of revolution. There is the far-eastern situation – Japan with a bayonet at the midriff of China, with Russia by no means a disinterested spectator. There are the tens of millions of unemployed in America and Europe, the precarious state of industry and agriculture, and the concentration of wealth in terms of money, to name only a few.

The year of grace 1932 is not going to set right all of these things, but there is a feeling abroad that a start has already been made and that conditions will gradually right themselves. One general prophesy can be made with confidence for the year in this respect – that 1932 will leave the condition of the world either considerably better or else a very great deal worse. There will be either a mending or a cracking of the wheel of civilization. Informed opinion is putting its money on the former.

*   *   *

The course of true prophesy does not always run smoothly. The prophet of shoals and rapids and troubles ahead has a thankless task and his forebodings generally go by the board and his reward is a sour look. When Reeve Scott predicted to his council in early 1930, when wheat was quoted on the exchange at $1.25, that next year the municipality would have to finance on 80 cent wheat – it is not recorded that he was given a vote of thanks. And when *The Times*, in the closing weeks of 1930, suggested a wholesale slashing of salaries and indemnities in the public service from the premier down, including teachers, the "hear, hear" was anything but vociferous. But wheat went well below 80c, and now salaries have perforce been slashed, although with bad grace and too late. – So when you feel like prophesying do it in a Pollyanna vein. People don't like the other kind.

*   *   *

Newspapers in Canada are making much of the discomfiture of Hon. E. C. Drury, former premier of Ontario, in the matter of his request for the unpaid balance of his salary as premier. While premier he declined to accept but $9,000 annually of his $12,000 salary. The difference has remained to his credit on the provincial books. Recently Mr. Drury asked for this money, and also asked that the matter be not made public. This latter request is what is proving so embarrassing to him – the construction placed on his action being that he wished to first publicly give away his "cake" then surreptiously reach out for it and eat it.

*   *   *

Two most significant events have transpired in Germany within the past few days. The first and more important is the budget which, for the first time since the signing of the Versailles Treaty, makes no provision for the payment of reparations. This may probably be construed as a notice to the world that Germany is through with the entire reparations folly. To date the Reich has borrowed from abroad just a little more than it has paid on reparations account. The creditor nations will not accept goods on account which, after all, is the only way international accounts can be paid. How the creditors will react to this notice is difficult to forecast; but the sooner they acknowledge that war debts must be wiped off the slate for the excellent reason that they cannot and will not be met, the better for all concerned. The second event is the re-election of Paul von Hindenburg to the presidency of the German republic with a clear majority of over half of the entire votes cast. The eighty-four year old general is elected to a term of seven years, and will thus be over ninety is he survives this term. Arrayed against him and the principles of moderation for which he stands, were the Fascism of Hitler and the Communism of Thaelmann. That the German people in their distress, which is acute, did not turn from Hindenburg and his moderation is further proof that always in times of moderate depression people turn to radical leaders and their promises of grand reforms, but if the depression be unduly prolonged and severe they turn back to the moderationists. This was borne out in Great Britain last year in the formation of a coalition government, in Germany last Sunday and in various parts of the world. It is evidence of fear, that people will rather bear the ills they have, if only they are bad enough, than fly to others of which their knowledge is but vague and theoretical.

*   *   *

One of the most spectacular cases of volte face the world has ever seen is undoubtedly that of Lloyd George, who has just issued a book ("The Truth About Reparations and War Debts") denouncing the Versailles Treaty he did so much to fashion. He is now the only one left alive of the Big Four (Lloyd George, Clemenceau, Wilson and Orlando) who drew the treaty, and it is a strange commentary on that tremendous folly that he should now rise to say that it should be scrapped. But Lloyd George is essentially forthright, and for all his dissembling as a politician, he has the courage of his convictions. Where a smaller man would have sought to lay the breakdown of reparations payments to other causes, Lloyd George makes no attempt to defend the treaty but recommends to the world its immediate scrapping and a frank acknowledge that war reparations are dead. "In my view, it is not worth while keeping afloat any part of the reparations debts. I am fully convinced that salvage operations to rescue any scrap from the deep into which it has sunk are not worth the cost and risk." He is seeing and acknowledging now, after a great deal of mischief has already been done, what should have been obvious at the outset – that reparations would not be paid on the scale laid down in the treaty for the excellent reason that they could not be paid. Keynes, Dillon and many others saw it, and pointed it out with all the force they could bring to bear, but to no avail. The victorious nations would continue to squeeze juice from the lemon long after the lemon was squeezed dry. On that theory they built up elaborate systems of international settlements. That theory has been fruitful of much mischief and is responsible in no small degree for the mess the world finds itself in today. That Lloyd George now so emphatically and courageously speaks his mind on the subject is a good omen of returning sanity after the postwar madness.

*   *   *

TaX marks the spot where the money was last seen.

*   *   *

Political and financial leaders in the U.S. are becoming thoroughly alarmed at the stubborn nature of the depression and are indulging in dire predictions of storms ahead unless courageous action is taken to cope with it. Within the past week two notable and influential men – Rainey, Democratic leader in Congress, the other being the owner of the *Chicago Tribune* – have publicly stated that the national government is bankrupt and that little short of revolution is ahead. As it is, the national government is spending nearly nine million dollars more than it collects every twenty-four hours. Taxes, national, state and county, already take one dollar of every $4.35 of the entire income of the people, which is over sixty billion annually, and it is hard to see how taxes can be increased to take up the present deficit under existing conditions. The machine of government has become top-heavy, due to bureaucracy. A Frankenstein monster has grown up to a stature where he can no longer be controlled. Just what is ahead is difficult to foresee. But the unmistakable signs are that a people numbering 120,000,000, whose vaults are crammed with gold, whom almost every nation on earth owes money, and whose granaries are bulging with food and materials, is on the verge of bankruptcy and starvation.

1933

This flight took place on Dec. 17, 1932 originating in Winnipeg at 11:00 a.m. and terminating in Treherne 55 minutes later, at 11:55, with passenger "Crosby."

O'ER HILL AND DALE

It was over a "spot" of that supreme catalyst of which Omar sang so eloquently that the matter was first broached. And when my good friend suggested that he fly me home in the morning I protested, albeit feebly, like the thrifty man at the luncheon date when his companion appropriates the checks. Knowing my predilection in the matter he said of course I could have the rear pit and the controls. This was indeed too much. Only the milling crowds about prevented me falling upon his neck in ecstasy.

In the morning following, it was not without a feeling of diffidence that I called him on the telephone to ask if he had made the offer in all seriousness. He had, and the machine would be ready whenever I was. And thus it came about that I was presently climbing into a close-fitting flying suit and a prodigious pair of fur-lined scows, plus helmet, face-mask and goggles, the ensemble having the appearance of a deep-sea diver. Thus accoutred I clambered into the pit of a pulsating Curtis Reid sesqui-plane which mechanics had "tuned" till it "percolated" to perfection (flying lingo is indeed as distinct as that peculiar to printing, and equally expressive) my good and most accommodating friend, equally warmly clad, stowing his elephantine bulk in the bare front pit.

Getting the all-clear signal, we taxied to the lee side of the field and headed into a stiff south-west wind. With "full-gun" she rose easily and by the time the Assiniboine was reached had an altitude of 1000 feet. The powerful Gipsy motor was functioning perfectly and the machine was gaining altitude steadily with the prop turning at cruising speed – some 300 per minute less than at take-off. Over Starbuck we had an altitude of 3000, which is a large safety margin in rural Manitoba at this time of year, when almost any field can afford an emergency landing. At this point I had finally got the hang of the stabilizer which had me puzzled at first as I no longer had to fight the machine. She now rode on an even keel without the suggestion of engine torque. (Unless equalized on the ailerons all single-motored planes in flight want to roll over on their backs by virtue of the thrust on the crankshaft.) Now Fannystelle was below and Culross and Elm Creek immediately ahead. These in turn slid by away below, toy towns with miniature stores and dwellings, flanked by postage-stamp fields, clear-cut and even. A minute or two (or so it seemed) and Haywood, St. Claude and Rathwell in turn were left behind.

During this latter stage of the journey it had puzzled me to find the machine drifting to the left. Again and again I had been obliged to yaw with a bank and turn to keep heading directly for the objective. The take-off had been into the teeth of a south-west wind, but this had evidently veered into the west or north-west. Now it is most important in landing to know the exact direction of the wind, not only to reduce speed by heading into it, but because landing cross-wind is to invite disaster by reason of the drift multiplying the strain on the under-carriage. In the absence of a ground air indicator ("sock") wind can often be determined by smoke from chimneys, the swaying of trees or drifting loose snow. Flyers will therefore often circle the field picked out for alighting, not only to study its nature and extent if unfamiliar but to make certain that the wind has not veered into another quarter since the take-off. So in this instance a few circles above the town while losing altitude showed the wind due west and a landing effected in the field west of town accordingly. Within a couple of minutes our good friend had climbed from the front to the rear pit and was off on the return journey. The outward passage had taken less than forty minutes, even against a breeze, and the gas consumed no more than a car would require to cover a like distance.

Truly the ideal way to travel, and most certainly the coming way. The time is not far distant when everybody will fly as a matter of course, many in their own machines as they now do in cars. Flying is becoming safer, pleasanter and faster with every passing year and its future is no more in doubt today than was that of automobiles in 1915.

* * *

During the past three years the Bracken government has spent $177 for every $100 received in tax revenue. Since 1929 it has borrowed $27,000,000, or more than the total debt as it stood in 1914. It has been borrowing to pay current expenses – rightly condemned as a major error in public finance.

* * *

One of the acts of the late parliament was to place an embargo on the imports of used light-planes from the U.S. Only craft above a certain very high cost is allowed entry, and this effectively bars the enterprising individual from buying any small craft for import into this country. It is no secret that the U.S. is far in the lead of other countries in the manufacture of light airplanes, and a few of these were coming in despite even the very high tariff and were cutting in on the trade of the large aerial transportation companies. This has now been effectively stopped (and it requires no Philadelphia lawyer to see at whose representation this has been brought about). So we have the anomaly of the government on the one hand subsidizing flying clubs, supplying them with inferior light planes of European make (costing far out of proportion to their intrinsic worth) and making cash grants to the clubs for every pilot trained, and on the other hand making it practically impossible for the pilot so trained to make use of his training by this ridiculous embargo. If it is the purpose of the government to promote civil aviation, as its aid to the flying clubs suggests, then this embargo effectively nullifies it. But apparently the large airways companies have spoken in the matter, and spoken to some purpose.

*   *   *

Irvin Cobb was once asked his opinion as to who won the war. He countered with another question; "Who won the San Francisco earthquake?" Too often the prize of the battlefield has no more substantial value than that. Everyone loses.

*   *   *

Aircraft CF-ARH

This aircraft, a high-wing monoplane, was built by the Pietenpol Aircraft Works in Minnesota and shipped to this country in parts and assembled by Mr. Maurice Fry, of Hartney, Manitoba, who had taken a course in aircraft lore in Minneapolis. It was designed by Mr. Pietenpol and is a standard Aircamper type of approved craft. The type has proved very satisfactory and is in wide use in the northern U.S. Its certificate of registration in this country is No. 1073, being inspected and passed by the Department of Civil Aviation for private use.

Legend: it has a span of 28 feet 2 inches and an overall length of 17 feet 8 inches. Height, 7 feet; weight empty, 680 lbs; authorized load 400 lbs. It is powered with a special type of in-line 4-cyl. motor using the Ford A block. It is sometimes referred to as Ford-powered, but this is the only Ford part used. Special pistons and crank-shaft, special high-compression head, special oiling and ignition systems designed at the Pietenpol factory are used. It develops about 40 h.p., which is very much higher than in many other light craft on the market. Normal cruising speed about 75 mph. Gas consumption, about 3 gals. per hour. Range, about 300 miles.

1933 – Bogi's plane, with registration CF-ARH, in front of the Treherne Times building. The plane was last heard of in the 1950s.

This type of craft is contended by many to be very suitable for the ambitious beginner as a training machine. The system used by many novice owners of such craft is to learn to handle the machine on the ground by taxiing at progressively increased speeds approaching the take-off speed. When this has been mastered (and any normal youngster can do it) a few lessons dual control with some competent instructor will enable the student to fly his own machine and in time acquire a pilot's license at very little cost.

It is the present purpose of *The Times* to offer this aircraft (or an alternative cash prize) as first prize in a subscription contest later during the present season, particulars of which will be announced in due time. This will afford some ambitious youngster here to break into the flying game by first acquiring his own craft, at little or no cost.

I have been unable to find the promised follow-up article but understand that the subscription-selling contest was won by Ted Kane, who promptly sold the aircraft to a resident of Brandon.

* * *

1999 – A Pietenpol Aircamper, constructed in 1965. This plane, which is kept in Edmonton, Alberta, carries the registration C-FARH.

The writer was recently privileged to witness a demonstration of television, this new and marvellous achievement of scientists whereby actual scenes can be mirrored at distances, much as sound is now carried from place to place either through wires or through the air. It left no doubt in his mind that television has now been achieved, despite crudities yet to be ironed out, and that it is one of the next major developments in the life of man. It is a natural corollary of the radio, and we feel quite secure in predicting that in but a few years it will be no less common and quite as perfect in its way as radio reception is today. Indeed, the principle is much the same, light in place of sound being translated into electric impulses and then translated back to the original form at the receiving end. While still in the experimental and evolutionary stage, and about as crude as radio reception was eight years ago, its possibilities are unquestioned. While the demonstration we witnessed left much to be desired, no one could be other than impressed with its future, and the tremendous influence its advent may have on future generations. As the human eye is, of all man's senses, the avenue by which he gathers most of his impressions, so perfected television is bound to enlarge his horizon, teach him, divert him and eventually may work profound changes in his mode of life as well as upon his outlook upon the world. – We are living in a time of almost kaleidoscopic changes, and tomorrow, in the figurative sense, may see changes which today we can but vaguely envision. Television is one such change, which is almost upon us.

*   *   *

Next Sunday, Dec. 17, just thirty years will have passed since man made his first flight in heavier-than-air craft, the first Wright brothers plane taking the air under its own power on that date at Kitty Hawk, South Carolina, in 1903. It wasn't much of a flight, lasting something less than one minute. But the significant element of that "hop," quickly realized the world over, was not how well or badly it flew, but that it flew at all.

The rest was merely a matter of experiment and development. It is a far cry from that first craft to Post's "Winnie Mae," which circumnavigated the globe twice, or the multi-motored clipper-ships of Pan American airways, weighing up to 35,000 lbs. and carrying scores of passengers on thousand mile hops. At that, man's conquest of the air is still in its first stages of development and is but an indication of future modes of travel unless, indeed, our civilization be on the brink of retrogression into barbarism, as former civilizations have collapsed. Barring this contingency, rocket ships will be cleaving the stratosphere at a thousand-miles-an-hour pace within the time of those now young.

1934

Readers of papers with an international outlook, who have the training or astuteness to read between the lines, will have noted the ominous undertone in press dispatches from Europe of late. Not since July of 1914 have war clouds looked so heavy and close as at this very moment. Almost all of Europe and some of the Orient appear to be on the brink of unutterable disaster. Central Europe is little more than an open powder barrel with sparks flying all around it. Austria, fearful – and not without cause – of being set upon by Germany is appealing to the League of Nations for protection. In France anything, not excepting internecine strife, may happen. Japan and Russia have "squared away" for action in Manchuria, and may be at it, tooth and nail, at any moment. In one recent tentative air raid over Russian territory Japan had six machines shot down. Some influence stepped in and the incident was not allowed to develop into open warfare – not even to get into the great news channels. But it is not the less significant. – To the student of history the present moment is packed with dynamite, with detonators in place. Commentators are agreed that it would take very little to plunge Europe into a war beside which the Great War was but mildly disastrous. Such are the prospects today.

* * *

Readers of this will recall a furor caused by a student group at Oxford University pledging that they would not fight for King or country if called upon to do so. Its sponsors were challenged by their betters to retract, but because those same betters lacked the persuasive influence of the thumb-screw and rack, they did not get the results of Galileo's examiners. Not a few were properly shocked at such conduct, wondering where today's young generation was heading. And well they might; for this same young generation itself has no idea of its direction. All it knows with certainty is that it doesn't care to trace the steps of passing and preceding generations. It has little respect for antecedents, viewing the mess the world has been brought to. And who can blame youth if its respect be of scant measure?

More recent, if no less significant, was the action of a class of Winnipeg college seniors declaring their loss of faith in democratic institutions and the capitalistic system, and vowing their intention to vote for dictatorship when the opportunity presents itself.

While neither the group at Oxford nor the seniors at Winnipeg are likely to change present forms of recruiting armies, their pronunciamentos voice a threat against the existing order. They are not important bodies, and their utterances are to be reckoned with only as they voice the sentiments and convictions of the numberless inarticulate. It is then that they gain weight and strength.

That the rising generation has little respect for the past and its traditions is understandable. The past – the recent no less than the distant – has little call to expect any large measure of respect from a generation left free to examine the records. The late war was the culmination of an era of vicious folly, and it was youth, who had no part in the shaping of that folly, that suffered. Recognizing the truth of that, why should not today's youth serve notice on the world, as did the group at Oxford, that it refuses to sacrifice itself in another culmination of folly? And seeing the trend of present democratic governments and the pass to which the world has come under their guidance, why should not a class of Winnipeg college students avow their lack of faith in such institutions and declare their desire for dictatorships?

Such things need surprise no one, much less create alarm. They are however, no less significant as a vane showing that today's youth is thinking, and thinking fearlessly and independently.

*   *   *

There is no investment in this world of ours that returns such high dividends in comfort and happiness and goodwill as a few moments devoted to the understandings of the other fellow's point of view.

*   *   *

Who would have thought, back in 1918, that Canada would officially decree that all flags on public buildings should fly at half-mast in honor of General Hindenburg on the day of his funeral! Tempus has a way of softening and modifying our emotions, even to our pet hates.

*   *   *

Times were different then. This is an item in the major newspaper in the province of a car accident on a highway more than a hundred miles west of Winnipeg. There were injuries of a minor nature, serious to those who sustained them, no doubt, but minor nonetheless. Father's car, being driven by Joe Forshere, was a nearly new Essex, an upscale automobile company which didn't survive the "Dirty Thirties." I remember the large chrome radiator cap from this car being on Father's desk at the office serving as an ashtray. Unfortunately it was one of the many items which did not make the move with us to Vancouver.

SEVEN INJURED IN COLLISION NEAR CYPRESS RIVER
Cars from Treherne and Glenboro Crash on Highway Friday Night

(SPECIAL DESPATCH TO THE FREE PRESS)

Cypress River, Man., July 16. – A head-on collision three miles east of here on No. 2 highway late Friday night resulted in injury to seven men. An automobile owned by Bogie Bjarnason, editor of the Treherne Times, and driven by Joe Forshere, with Ted Kane in the back seat, all of Treherne, collided with a car owned by Elwood Cartmell, of Glenboro, and carrying Jack Oleson, of Winnipeg; Jack Wilson and John Bjornson, of Glenboro.

Cartmell claims that the Treherne car was running without lights and following close behind a big truck and the Glenboro car, after passing the truck, cut back on the highway and the two cars crashed with a two foot overlap. John Bjornson is in bad shape with a smash on the top of his head and his face wounded in several places. The Treherne publisher also fared badly with a hole through his mustache.

Kane got a nasty scalp wound while Forshere got off with a cut on the arm and chest injury. Wilson had his head and face cut badly. Cartmell has nasty face and scalp gashes. Oleson got off with a scratch on the face.

It is stated that the Treherne men were returning from Brandon about 11 o'clock and had reached a point just east of the gravel pit when the Glenboro car came from the east, cut in around a truck and pinned them. The left front corners of both cars are a complete wreck. Both steering wheels are broken and glass shattered all around.

The Glenboro injured were brought into town in a truck from Baldur that came along, and received first aid from Nurse Faulkner, there being no doctor in town. Bjornson's case was considered too serious to deal with here, so he was rushed to Glenboro. The Treherne men were taken to Treherne by a passing car.

The "Winnipeg Free Press" may have been the leading daily newspaper in the province but it produced writing that would not have been tolerated in a small weekly paper printed in Treherne.

*   *   *

Man proposes but does not invariably dispose. Chance and circumstance may at any time intervene to upset the applecart. Two weeks back I closed this column with the words, "See you next week." That proved a rash promise, for "next week" I didn't "see you" at all, the range of vision out of one tortured eye being limited to what an ordinary bedroom affords. I hadn't reckoned with Friday the 13th and the looming of a swift chariot out of the darkness. It brought a jolt, some discomfort and inconvenience and property loss and no end of other results, among them some questions.

Considering the subject of motor traffic on our highways in general some inconsistencies are encountered. Practically anybody with the means can purchase and licence a powerful car. The government obliges with fine all-weather highways and is itself a partner in vending intoxicants at convenient stations along these highways. The licensee is admonished not to drive to the public danger, but until he comes a cropper there is little let to what he may do on the public thoroughfare.

Now while alcohol in certain forms may be excellent in the fueltank of a car, its influence on the other side of the accelerator is of questionable merit. Even in small quantities it may dull the driver's sense of danger and responsibility and at the same time detract from his alertness and efficiency. A pilot of an airplane discovered to be ever so little under its influence would be summarily disqualified, but the motorist in charge of a machine no less capable of being a public menace goes his merry way.

There would seem to be need of compulsory insurance to be carried by all motor licensees to the effect that any victim, either in person or property, of his inefficiency or recklessness may be assisted. Indeed, truck licensees are now required to be so bonded, and this might be readily be extended to all holders of motor vehicle licenses.

It is, of course, regrettable that the large body of financially responsible and at once capable and careful motorists should be required to carry such insurance wholly because a few irresponsible and at once reckless licensees continue to be public menaces on our highways. Yet this is the rule in society, for its own protection, that all must bear in some measure the penalties of its evildoers. So far we have not devised ways to obviate this.

The preceding item was some pages removed in the scrapbook but surely referred to the accident described above.

*   *   *

The figure of Justice with her scales is always pictured as blindfolded. The man in the street reading accounts of the dispensing of justice may sometimes be justified in lamenting her blindness and wishing that she might be less impartial in her decrees. Thus we read with mingled feelings that at one sitting of court at Russell, Manitoba, recently, a motorist was fined $2 for approaching a highway without pausing, running into three loads of hay, one of which upset causing serious injury to the man in charge, while two other men were each fined $50 for having purchased liquor illegally. It may be assumed that these fines were according to the letter of the law, and probably the judge had no choice. The reckless driver who caused grave injury to another and endangered the lives of at least two more was fined $2 while the men who indiscreetly bought bottles of liquor were each fined $50. Law, doubtless; but not justice.

*   *   *

The boy in the teen age is a strange creature - if not quite so strange as a grown-up. In most cases his main ambition is to get over the period with all possible dispatch, presumably in the belief that adults are having all the fun, since they are not hedged about with the restrictions imposed on the youngster with the end in view of saving him from himself. He wants to be a man, free to do as he likes in all things, in the fond belief that the adult enjoys this privilege, and to achieve at least a semblance of this he tries to emulate sophistication and the devil-may-care attitude he ascribes to manhood. In most cases this is a phase of the struggle for self-preservation, a foil to the inferiority complexes which beset him, a result of unskilful leading of the part of his elders to whom he unconsciously looks for guidance. It may truly be said that the boy is one part heredity and two parts environment, and if the sum is no credit to himself it is much less so to his betters. But strangest of all is the fact that while most men have passed through the difficult teen-age period (there are exceptions to this as to most other things) the adult can rarely understand the boy. He cannot get it through the adamant of his understanding that today's teen-age boy might just possibly be somewhat like yesterday's boy. In rare lucid moments the adult will hark back to acknowledge that he was himself somewhat wild and prone to dally with the forbidden, but if he sees evidences of this tendency in his own son he will declare that the rising generation is on the high-road to hell. – All of which is passing strange and true.

*   *   *

One thing the radio is doing – it is familiarizing listeners (which includes almost everyone in these parts) with the proper pronunciation of the names of foreigners in the news, and of musicians of our day and of days that are gone. In most cases announcers are scrupulously correct in this respect (although slip-ups occur, as with the name of the Italian dictator; no properly-schooled Italian would say "Moos," as most announcers do). Which is all to the good. There is now no longer any excuse for pronouncing Mozart or Beethoven or Verdi phonetically. Most unfortunately this rule is not being carried out in the matter of foreign place names. Canadian and U.S. announcers persist in using Anglicized versions of names of European continental countries and cities. Often these versions are pointless and senseless corruptions, in cases so far-fetched that a native of the country or city named might experience difficulty in recognizing what is meant. Why not use native pronounciation and spelling in the case of place-names? By what right do we say Rheims, or Copenhagen, or Hungary, or, for that matter, Paris or Brussels – like that? Or our own Montreal, which we do not come within a mile of pronouncing correctly? A foreigner to Manitoba or Saskatchewan could with equal right say windbag for Winnipeg and articulate the g hard in Regina. We would consider both gratuitous license and put it down to "foreign" dumbness. Yet we (and this includes radio announcers) do this every day in respect to foreign place-names, and think nothing of it, probably on the assumption that if "Foreigners" persist in giving their cities "outlandish" names we have every right to re-name them.

*   *   *

1935

"I do not agree with a word that you say, but I will defend to the death your right to say it." That was Voltaire, stormy petrel of eighteenth century France, intellectual liberator extraordinary and father of the French revolution. No single sentence could describe him so well as this; for much as he raged against things as he found them, saying so in ninety and nine volumes of fiery denunciation, he was above all tolerant of everything save intolerance. Raging, he unleashed the forces that culminated in the revolution and the corollary Napoleonic wars. That he could not forsee what was to follow is not to his discredit. He merely sowed the wind and the world reaped the whirlwind.

Voltaire came on the scene at a time when France was rotten with the corruption of a dissolute monarchy and court, ably abetted by a church still vested with inquisitorial powers and desperately anxious to maintain things as they were, even to celebrating the anniversary of the St. Bartholemew massacre. It took courage to beard those two in their own strongholds; but Voltaire did, and to such good purpose that neither dared silence him peremptorily. The Bastille was tried, then exile – England, Prussia, Switzerland. All the while he poured out a veritable Niagara of propaganda against superstition and corruption.

On his funeral car, followed by 100,000 men and women while 600,000 others flanked the streets of Paris to do him honor, were the words; "He gave the human mind a great impetus; he prepared us for freedom." And because of him the storm was loosed when and as it came. The world was never the same again, despite such setbacks as the first Napoleon, because he had sown the seed of intellectual freedom that had taken root. Such work is never entirely in vain. With Voltaire France began to think – explosively. Louis XVI, seeing in his temple prison the works of Voltaire and Rousseau, said, "Those two men have destroyed France" – meaning his dynasty; which was as far as a Bourbon could see. "After me the deluge" applied not to a Louis but to Voltaire.

Because of his forthright language Voltaire has often been classed as an atheist and destroyer of religion. It is true that he asked searching questions and did not always display the cringing attitude his times demanded, as when he insisted that if the bishop hear his confession he would hear the bishop's confession. Nor did such passages as the following enhance his reputation for piety. – "Nobody thinks of giving an immortal soul to the flea; why then to an elephant, or a monkey, or my valet? ... To rise again – to be the same person that you were – you must have your memory; for it is memory that makes your identity; the only part of you that has survival value. If your memory be lost, how will you be the same again? ... Why do mankind flatter themselves that they alone are gifted with a spiritual and immortal principle? ... Perhaps from their inordinate vanity. I am persuaded that if a peacock could speak he would boast of his soul, and would affirm that it inhabited his magnificent tail."

Essentially Voltaire was a deeply religious man, but the distinction between superstition and religion was fundamental with him. He said; "I adore God, love my friends, do not hate my enemies, and detest superstition." Being far ahead of his time that was not enough, and so he was denied Christian burial and to the church his name has been anathema. But his influence has been tremendous, and always for freedom and the well-being of man.

*   *   *

How far removed the capitalistic tinkers of the Bennett, Roosevelt type are from beginning to understand the ailments that beset us is exemplified in the decision of the Bennett government to print the voters lists in the federal printing plant at Ottawa. With tens of millions of dollars worth of printing machinery standing idle throughout the 245 constituencies and with thousands of printers idle and many on relief, the government set about to save money by importing batteries of typesetting machines and presses to enable the central printing plant to do work which in the very nature of things should have been distributed throughout all the ridings and thus set money circulating for the revival of business. The big problem is to keep money circulating – to get it into the hands of the masses to pass along for shoes and sugar and the thousand necessities of everyday life. To "save" money in the way described above is the surest way to lose double in doles to idle and indigent men, eating their hearts out for something to turn to while a few at

Ottawa work day and night at high pressure for a very problematical saving. The tragedy of that is not only that printers everywhere (except in Ottawa) are done out of work and money which is rightfully theirs, but in the realization that the government has not begun to understand what is at the root of our troubles and what is required to begin the process of recovery, if that is still possible.

* * *

Whatever it was that was taking place in far Palestine about nineteen hundred years ago – and what that was is not very clear to us, despite the voluminous literature surrounding it – it was something that has made a deeper impress upon western civilization than any other one thing since time began. The son of a humble village carpenter went about for a year or so among equally humble folk and told them homely truths, only to run foul of the priesthood of his own people and so was obligingly put to death by the Roman authorities in the usual manner, at a time when such executions were daily occurances. There is reason to think that it made but little stir at the time, for contemporary records ignore it, and for two to three hundred years it lived only in oral tradition; but the seeds of a tremendous moral upheaval were taking root. Now, as Passion week is being observed, nineteen centuries after the event, the full significance of that tragic drama is better realized.

"The two and seventy jarring sects" continue at outs about the precise meaning of the life and teachings of the Nazarene Carpenter. Not a village in all Christendom but has the proponents of many varying interpretations of the meaning of the Man and His mission. But all are in tacit agreement about the tremendous influence His words and example have wielded from that day to this.

* * *

About the time that Western Europe was developing the strange mass insanity which found expression in the Crusades and culminated in the horrors of the Inquisition, a Persian tent-maker by the name of Omar Khayyam was composing disjointed verses of singular quality and haunting beauty. A philosopher-scientist (his avocation was astral mathematics), he speculated on the matter uppermost in men's minds – the relation of man and God and man and the universe in the light of prevailing knowledge and religions. His findings and philosophy are expressed in the collection of quatrains called the Rubaiyat, so beloved of scholars everywhere.

Discovered by the Anglo-Irish scholar Fitzgerald about the middle 19th century his translation of the collection met with a chilly reception from the editors and publishers of his day. A privately printed first edition of 200 copies found buyers only when reduced to two pence a copy. But of a sudden people woke up to the startling beauty and originality of thought in the 101 stanzas of the poem and Omar and Fitzgerald became a vogue, almost a cult. To this day the Rubaiyat maintains the high esteem it then won among scholars and lovers of the beautiful in belles lettres, and few things are more often quoted.

A Muslim by upbringing Omar was no stranger to the teachings of Christianity and other religions. In the crucible of his keen mind he compares and sifts and drenches them in the acid of intellect. He finds some pure metal but when he has cleared away the dross and trappings not enough is left to buy the immortality so engagingly promised by all. If there is something to choose between them he doesn't think there is enough to go to war about, and he is inclined to treat the matter lightly. He sheds the currently held fear and liberates his intellect from the nightmare of a petulant deity. Likewise – and in this his originality is most striking – he connects cause and effect, which most in his and many in our day are unable to do where religion is concerned. Hence his embarrassing questions, as unanswerable now as then, but usually glossed over in discourse with a skill and technique born of long practice.

Below are a few specimens:

> What! out of senseless Nothing to provoke
> A conscious Something to resent the yoke
>   Of unpermitted Pleasure, under pain
> Of Everlasting Penalties, if broke!
>
> What! from this helpless Creature be repaid
> Pure Gold for what he lent him dross-allay'd
>   Sue for a Debt he never did contract,
> And cannot answer – Oh the sorry trade!
>
> But helpless Pieces of the Game He plays
> Upon this Checker-board of Nights and Days;
>   Hither and thither moves, and checks, and slays,
> And one by one back in the Closet lays.

There is music as distinct in a quatrain of Khayyam as in a melody by Schubert. But if he appeals to the sense of beauty his challenge to the intellect is no less arresting, and no man worthy of a study of the Rubaiyat can read it without enriching his mind and being mentally stimulated. More, he can go back to it again and again and yet again and each time be conscious of its eternal freshness, its message and its beauty. Omar has been styled "the prophet of pessimism," but this is scarcely just. He is merely honest and expresses with directness what to him is the truth.

> When You and I behind the Veil are past,
> Oh, but the long, long while the World shall last,
>   Which of our Coming and Departure heeds
> As the Seas's self should heed a pebble cast.

*   *   *

Advanced Mathematics

Problem – To add: "No country, no Empire, has a greater desire for peace than our country and our Empire." – Stanley Baldwin.

Plus: "This Government, like the French people, is profoundly attached to peace." – Pierre-Etienne Flandin.

Plus: "What could I wish but peace and quiet?" – Adolf Hitler

Plus: "The greatest need of the world today is the assurance of permanent peace." – Franklin D. Roosevelt.

And to obtain the following result (reported by the League of Nations' new Armaments Year Book): Cost of world armaments increases by $500,000,000 in 1934.

*   *   *

Aviation: – Here then is the field of endeavor to which today's youth should be directing its attention. There is scope and opportunity for all, an unlimited field for study and experiment. The young man here as elsewhere, biting his nails for lack of place and opportunity in a world grown suddenly too small, can now literally look up and take heart. There is a place for him in the blue of the upper reaches if he prepares for it. The British government alone is opening recruiting offices to add 2,500 pilots and 20,000 ground men to its air force (for normally it takes a score of men on the ground to keep one plane in the air.) Commercial aviation is merely in its fledgling stage compared with what is ahead.

So, young man, interest yourself in aviation; become air-minded. There is much to learn, so be about it. It is challenging work, and worthy of the best that you can give to it. The second third of the 20th century, barring the breakdown of civilization, will see the advancement of flying comparable only with that of motoring in the first third. The manufacture, operation and servicing of aircraft will demand its tens of millions of experts in all its branches. And the time to prepare is NOW!

*   *   *

1936

Only two classes of men can view the current European scene without experiencing something akin to "the jitters." They are (a) the very brave, and (b) the very stupid. The poor rest of us who are neither one nor the other, but dwell in the shades and borderlands, are at this time normally verging on panic lest what passes for peace over there be shattered and the powers fly at each others throats. For if we are relatively remote from the actual theatre of any European or African or Mediterranean conflict, we cannot hope to be unaffected by it, and the chances are far more than even that we will be drawn into it. And anyone who can contemplate with equanimity the prospect of getting tangled up in a modern large-scale war either knows very little about war or his mind functions along lines not given the ordinary or garden variety of man.

Consider the scene. Here is Italy, dominated by an ambitious individual given to direct methods, now engaged in a venture in East Africa that seems, on the surface at least, to cut across all lines of international morality. Here is Germany, arming to the teeth with a thoroughness which bodes ill for tranquillity, particularly of those who framed the Versailles Treaty. Here is France, nervous lest she again become the battleground. Across the Channel lie the British Isles whence threads extend to the ends of the earth, any of which may easily be the means of carrying the spark of universal conflict. To the east is Russia, intent upon her own affairs at the moment but a neighbor to be reckoned with if the balance be broken. Around and in between these powers are the numerous little entities, each steeped in intense nationalism, and potentially dangerous as nests of intrigue and incubators of hatreds and jealousy. In the far east is Japan, python-like swallowing China, four times as large and populous as itself and crowding the Russian Bear, the while thumbing its nose at the world and defying all and sundry at the London naval conference.

* * *

(The following was written by the conductor of this column shortly after the Great War, and headed "The Greater Faith." It is reprinted here because the arguments advanced have the same bearing today.)

It used to be said during the war that a new religion would issue from the trenches – the old revivified and purged, clear and with a new meaning. That inarticulate mass, the army, knee-deep in mud and locked in a conflict to the death, was thinking. That thought, we were told, was to crystalize into a simple and vital religion, the eternal verities of the old brought home and shorn of the trappings that muddle.

That happy issue has not yet come to pass. The same army, now in "civies" is still knee-deep in the mud of controversy, in conflict under banners of a multitude of creeds.

The soldier of the line did not concern himself greatly about his chances in a world to come, or even the possibility or probability of further life in the event of getting "bumped off." Left to himself he gave the matter no thought. In effect it was immaterial to him.

Cornered, and forced to express himself on the subject, he would declare himself in effect a fatalist; but he preferred not to talk about it. Innumerable Y.M.C.A. secretaries were at their wits' ends to "save the souls of the boys." They gave them tracts and sold them tea; and there are times, when the souls of men are tried, that a cup of tea is worth a mountain of tracts. But the Y men didn't know, then, and have not yet learned.

But if the soldiers were indifferent to the technical means of saving their souls it was through no lack of faith. Attribute it, rather, to a lack of fear, and to the feeling that justice would be done.

That attitude argues a greater and more worthwhile faith in God. They expected to be justly dealt by at the Mercy Seat; they asked for nothing more. They trusted God, and were willing to abide by His judgement, without attempting to pre-empt a bias in their favor by technical means, granted that possibility.

There is something wrong with that man's faith in the goodness of God who is forever on the "qui vive" lest his soul lack the letter-perfect credentials, should death unexpectedly claim him. He looks to his indenture, that it be properly sealed and executed. His rascally soul may not be worthy: but he will hold God to His bond.

The soldier rose above that in the ordeal. His was the greater faith.

* * *

Last week the giant new German Zeppelin, Von Hindenburg, returning from a trip to Buenos Aires, South America, on her maiden voyage, developed motor trouble, and was experiencing difficulty against headwinds. Off Gibralter she radioed a request to the French government for permission to take a direct route to the home port at Lake Constance over France instead of going the long way around by the North Sea or over the Mediterranean and the Italian Alps. The request was at first refused, but second and better thoughts prevailed and another message to the ship gave the requested permission. The giant airship, with over a hundred persons aboard, was spared the difficult trans-Alpine passage with two of its four motors crippled. In the night it sailed up the French Rhone Valley and in the morning moored safely to its home mast at Friedrichshafen. Not only that, but French air beacons were alight and ground crews stood by all night prepared to assist if the need arose.

Another and a greater ship by far is in distress – the great ship of European stability, holding the world's hope of peace. It is battling heavy headwinds, its motors stalling, its crew at outs as to direction and methods of navigation. Its cargo is not a mere handful of lives, however precious, but millions and millions. Should the headwinds of hate and fear and distrust bring it down the lethal gas of its great bag will spread death and desolation over not only Europe but over the entire world.

But now the appeals for aid are not so readily responded to. The Rhone Valley is not alight with beacons to give it direction. There is quarrelling and quibbling, barricaded borders. Yet this is surely another ship in distress. Will humanity rise equal to the occasion and aid it back to port? It may, but at the time of writing this it appears doubtful.

*　　*　　*

While much has been accomplished already the future of aviation is almost limitless. For this reason it is the field for the young man with ambition. The opportunities are endless, despite the fact that only four in a hundred can ever make good fliers. It takes many men and much equipment and organization to keep one machine in the air and it is in this organization that the future of the greater number lies.

Aviation is not only the coming mode of transportation, it is also the field of endeavor for the forward looking young man.

1937

Another year. And during the lull following the year-end festivities the world has been taking stock of its progress during the preceding twelve-month, as per age-old custom. What the reconciliation statements disclose may be gathered from sundry items of news, often seemingly unrelated, in the press. It is through these that the sighs and the "whoops" of a disappointed or a glad world may be detected, coming as they do unconsciously and from the heart.

We read about very definite improvements in trade and commerce, notably in the Americas, with a greater flow of money among the masses and more employment. To balance this are the ominous statements that there are greater numbers (in Canada) on relief rolls than at the same time last year, with serious and widespread industrial unrest in the U.S. However these may be interpreted, the seaman's and automotive worker's strikes are portents of no small significance. A bright spot is the increase in demand from abroad for Canadian agricultural products, notably wheat, for the time being disposing of the burdensome surplus that has weighted the markets in the past six years. This will undoubtedly be followed next summer by an increased acreage under wheat and a more hopeful outlook for agriculture. All of which is to the good.

Looking overseas the picture is more disturbing. The Orient is a bubbling caldron that may boil over at any moment. Europe is an armed camp, every nation ready to fight any or every other nation at the drop of the hat. That no major power has so far dropped the hat is said to be due to the general fear that a melee may result; and you don't always emerge the victor in a fight of that nature. Half-hungry and hopeless peoples are kept in line by totalitarian governments invoking ancient penalties (such as the death penalty in Germany for sending money out of the country), and by keeping a good percentage of the men under military discipline and armed. Another sizable portion of each nation is kept busy and so out of direct mischief, making armaments and at other unproductive work. However badly that may portend for the future, the immediate present is saved from general insurrection, but at the cost of mounting debts and a fear that war is inevitable. Indeed, the Spanish conflict is bringing this war so near that comfort and security are at the vanishing point.

And so the world passes another milestone on its spinning way. Some will say that mankind is not learning its lessons effectively or to profit by them, that it is indeed beyond being instructed by experience. Nineteen centuries of the Christian era, and the world's chief occupation is still war and preparation for war! A telling commentary, that, on our boasted progress.

*   *   *

If it is not quite an institution with us, this matter of spending a day in "The House" (the Manitoba Assembly) each year during the Throne-speech debate, it approaches being a habit. So on Friday we made the annual pilgrimage, wedging into the gallery facing the opposition benches shortly before three o'clock. We noted that Moses and Solon still hold up brazen admonishing fingers above the "distinguished visitors" benches and the frescoed ladies still cavort in scandalous and unseasonable attire, while chains still guard the main doors. So doubtless the general situation is still in hand and secure, whatever Manitoba bonds are being currently quoted.

And now honorable members drifted in, bowing as they faced the Chair. The mace was laid on the table and Mr. Speaker declared the house in session. But if there was any praying it escaped us. Mr. Willis (from a distorted gallery view reminding us forcibly of a Faust-character poster seen long ago) rose to ask about curling returns. A back-bencher volunteered the information that Mr. Aberhart's Alberta was whipping the tar out of Manitoba. Well, there didn't seem to be anything to be done about it beyond alasing, so Mr. Hyman rose in his place to present proof of corrupt election practices by government forces – offering refreshments at a political rally, for which the law specifies penalties of fines and imprisonment. Hon. Bracken and Hon. Major refuted this but Hyman read advertisements in both the Tribune and Free Press to this effect. The matter cleared up somehow, maybe by blaming the printers, and presently General Ketchen was holding forth.

The General, who could readily play the Earl Kitchener of 1915, was in a mood for compliments – at first. He complimented the speaker on his appointment, adding that there must surely be something in the Dauphin air that produced speakers (who, by the way, rarely speak). He complimented the house on having a lady member and said lady member on having a house to sit in and listen to speeches. All very complimentary. But he soon ran out of compliments or things to bestow them on and was saying that things, including Manitoba, were in a bad way thanks to the government or something. He digressed to say that he had spent a dollar, currency of the realm (despite his North-of-England origin and traditions) for an Alberta "prosperity certificate" which he displayed to a fascinated house. He had exchanged a bank's "promise to pay on demand" for an Alberta "promise to pay," both of the same denomination, and we gathered that he felt himself the loser, for the latter read "in two years" whereas the former was "on demand." (Is the General aware that bank and Dominion notes promise to "pay" only in renewals of promises to pay? That's a thought for him to ruminate on.)

Another sortie was when he noted that Labor was now C.C.F.-Labor, "with the accent on the hyphen." Which brought NO Hyman to his feet to ask whether the accent should be on the hyphen in pronouncing "Liberal-Conservative." – Just one of the little amenities, you know; tit for tat and all that.

And now the General was into his stride, no longer complimenting. The government was making a botch of things and he just didn't like it nohow. Words to that effect, anyway. (It's hard to hear up in the gallery, for this is indeed an acoustical chamber of horrors.)

Nearly two hours of this, and we noted that other honorable members were paying scant attention. At least half the original number had drifted out, and those remaining wore an air of languid indifference. Most of them were reading or engaged in conversation. It must indeed be VERY discouraging to hold forth under such conditions! And up in the press gallery, under the collective aegis of Confucius, Lycurgus, Alfred and Justinian, J.B.M. sat reading the Meditations of Marcus Aurelius, or maybe the Police Gazette. Anyway, he was reading, or knitting, or something.

So the afternoon wore away, and as we trudged down The Mall we glanced back at Kelly's magnificent pile and noted that the Golden Boy whom Time has tarnished to a dull copper, is still poised for his sprint, torch and sheaf and all. But the broken glass in the front door, that so used to rile T.B.R., has been replaced. Maybe it's a sign of something or other, like keeping the well-known wolf out. We like to leave that thought with you.

*　　*　　*

As a rule this column is written with an eye to the six or eight persons known to read it regularly, of the twenty-five or so hundred who see the paper every week. But now and again evidences come to hand that an odd reader beyond the faithful half-dozen scan it, at least occasionally. How else account for the blasts against it from the least expected quarters? Frequently readers take umbrage at statements made or find themselves impelled to offer corrections. For instance, some weeks back this column deplored the fact that Moses or Whoever wrote Exodus had written "Thou shalt not suffer a witch to live," stating that these words had brought much grief and suffering to the world. A reader challenges this statement and gives it as his opinion that the author of Exodus was justified in his dictum. And this being a nation where no Hitler or Mussolini is so far dictating what we shall think or say, this objector is entitled to say whatever he may desire about Moses and witches, and about this column.

About the time this blast was received a book, "Witchcraft and the Black Art," by J. W. Wickwar, considered an authority in the matter, came to the notice of this writer. It states that during the reign of Henry III, 30,000 witches were burned in France. Further: "In fifty years 100,000 witches were consigned to the flames in Germany. England, Scotland, Ireland, Spain all have a similar gruesome record. One authority estimates the total number of witches killed in Europe at 9,000,000."

A fairly gruesome set of figures, any way you look at them. Think of all the misery and terror, the heartaches, even among those who escaped with their lives but saw friends and relatives victims of the witch-hunters! Think of even the little town of Salem, in Massachusetts, U.S. where as late as 1690, no less than twenty hapless women were killed as witches in one year – a small town at that! What do you think life in Treherne would be like if the local authorities tried local housewives for witch-craft at the rate of one every two weeks or so and hanged them on Front Street for the edification of the rest? All that was re-quired was for someone to denounce a woman as having the "evil eye," or to be seen moving the lips silently. The accused had no defence; once she was "denounced," hanging or burning at the stake followed inevitably.

All this because a writer thousands of years back wrote an unfortunate sentence – "Suffer not a witch to live." Let our friend who disliked the column's reference to it some weeks back ponder the matter, and glean from the history of witch-hunting what comfort he can.

*   *   *

Whenever the occasion suggests it, and sometimes when it doesn't, U.S. and Canadian statesmen and orators generally, take deep breaths and launch upon the subject of the 3000 miles (isn't it 5000?) boundary separating the two nations without a single gun or soldier facing either way. This admirable condition is supposed to indicate something or other – that no immediate warfare is contemplated by either party and that neither has se-rious designs on the liberty or territory or chattels of the other. Which is all very fine, so far as it goes. Unfortunately this is not the whole of the picture. For if there are no guns nor soldiers nor even the familiar barbed-wire fences marking European boundaries, there are barriers no less potent in stemming the flow of trade. If Canadian consumers wish to purchase something made more economically in the U.S. they are obliged to pay handsome tribute in impost because some Canadian industry demands "protection." This is at times not merely irksome but also very expensive, and is apt to suggest anything but a cheer to the victim when he hears the "undefended boundary" mentioned. For if this boundary is not patrolled by armed guards, it is no less effectively manned by an army terrible with banners of tariff schedules, dedicated to harassing whatever commerce may attempt to flow forth or back.

Out of this arise thoughts – quite idle thoughts – of what would transpire if governments of the two nations got together and agreed to remove all restrictions, duties, quotas, etc., at this boundary, allowing goods, men and capital to flow back and forth without let or restriction or question of any kind whatsoever. Quite certainly there would be an immediate and colossal movement of men and materials both ways, if principally northward. Prices in Canada of manufactured goods would undergo drastic revision downward, on such things as agricultural implements, cars, household goods and many articles of food and clothing. There would be a vast expansion of business in most lines, with the influx of people and the opening of new areas. The population of Canada would double in a few years.

Balanced against this would be the insurgence of U.S. "culture" in Canada and danger to the British connection. Whether this latter would necessarily follow may be a matter of opinion. History does not seem to show that the freeing of trade between nations is particularly dangerous to national status. How it would affect business and industries now established and enjoying the protection of high tariffs is another matter. Many of these would find themselves faced with ruinous price competition and compelled to adjust themselves to it or go under. Not a few of these are uneconomic as it is and could not survive.

However, these are idle speculations, for free trade between the two principle nations on this continent is not likely to come about for a very long time.

*   *   *

Recent utterances of old world statesmen, notably Hitler, Mussolini and a Japanese spokesman, arising out of protests against aggression in Ethiopia, Spain, China, have been more than arresting in their cold-blooded realism. They have said to the world in general and Great Britain in particular: Yes, we mean to take what we want – so what? No such words, of course; but the meaning is just that. Mussolini and General de Bono in a new book on the conquest of Ethiopia are quite frank, in a boastful way, about that gruesome affair. Japan sends an armed force into the heart of a neighbor country and then finds a cause for war in the resistance offered. Spain is being bled white (a million slain in a year's fighting) by foreign troops on her soil, where they have no business to be that an observer at this distance can see.

To protests against such methods the reply, in effect is: You should talk! This has been your own modus operandi in the past. Now that you have all the land you want, taken in just this fashion, you have grown moral where others are concerned.

Which is, of course, stingingly true. The powers in the past have been doing without compunction just what Italy did in Ethiopia and what Japan is doing in North China. In international affairs the weak has always been at the mercy of the strong, and that mercy has been tempered only by expediency. A survey of history suggests that morality in international dealings has been practically non-existent. The principle of "Let him take who has the power and let him keep who can" has been and still is the method whereby the powers have been guided to gain and hold possession and might.

Acknowledgment of this leads inevitably to the conclusion that man and mankind, the individual and society, are ruled and restrained in their dealings one with another entirely by fear of the consequences. John Doe, Treherne farmer, is prevented from crossing the pike and forcibly annexing neighbor Richard Roe's land and chattels, knowing that he can do so with his more numerous sons and larger stock of pitchforks, only by the fear (in this case the certain knowledge) that Constable Powers and Magistrate Law would soon be asking him embarrassing and pointed questions about it. He knows also that in this they would have the backing of his other neighbors who would fear the example and consequences if his actions went unpunished. The stronger nations, knowing that they can "get away with it," because there is no higher court to fear, have no such restraints upon them. So they help themselves to what they want and then thumb their noses at the world and ask, in the diplomatic equivalent, "So What?"

That's how far we have come in the development of international morality in the six thousand (or is it six million?) years that man has inhabited the earth.

* * *

He is indeed a rare optimist who, when he stops to consider the international scene, is not assailed by waves of fear and despondency, borne in upon him with news from the four corners of the world. There are those who assert, with varying degrees of authority and of confidence, that there will be no world war, in the sense which that term generally conveys, in the near future because the major western powers do not want it and are not prepared for it. But wars have been and are raging in several sections of the world, and what is more sinister, the powers are aligning along clear-cut lines for the conflict which they believe must inevitably come. All are arming with feverish haste at a cost staggering in its immensity. Britain with its seven-and-a-half billion dollar armaments program is in deadly earnest about the necessity for readiness when the time comes for Mussolini to challenge for Mediterranean supremacy. That is no longer an ugly dream to be dismissed like a nightmare of an uncomfortable moment, but a fact so grim and of such startling inevitability that it cannot be forgotten or even shoved aside in the Christmas festivities now at hand, but persists in sitting like a specter even at the festive board.

No seventh-son wisdom is required to see how the powers will line up, now that the Rome-Berlin-Tokyo axis is an established fact. Against this combination is ranged the major European bloc comprised of Gt. Britain, France and Russia, the smaller nations casting their lots with one or the other according to the exigencies of the moment, their geographical positions, but mostly on how they will "bet on the winner." What such a conflict will be like may be gauged from the manner in which wars in Ethiopia, Spain and the Orient have been waged with the minimum of regard for civilian life and with a ferocity to be matched only with that of half-civilized vandals of the Dark Ages. Thus far have we come, and such is the outlook, after nineteen hundred years of exhortation to love one's neighbor as oneself! The Japanese have copied our methods but rejected for the most part the religion we have so consistently offered them. And now that the anniversary of the birth of Christianity is at hand, it is interesting to note that the most bellicose of all the earth's peoples harbors the nerve-center of the most powerful of the bodies of Christianity – Roman Catholicism – and that this, with other arms of the church, is either unwilling or powerless to stem the rising tide of destruction. Yet it must know that it too must go down in the ruins of civilization.

Not a very pleasant prospect; but what other prognosis of the Shape of Things to Come can be arrived at on the basis of the present state of the world?

1938

The Great War is over. Witness: Wilhelm Rodde, German Consul, is attending the convention of the Canadian Legion, B.E.S.L., at Fort William, this week, on a personal invitation from Brigadier General Alex Ross, the president. And last week on the occasion of the ex-German Kaiser's 79th birthday His Majesty King George VI sent his felicitations in the names of

"Bertie, May and Elizabeth" (himself, and Queens Mary and Elizabeth).

*   *   *

To say that the world is "jittery" over recent developments in Europe is to put it mildly, for these have been sinister indeed. With Hitler shouting his defiance at all and sundry, with Mussolini strutting and snapping his fingers, with Japan about to over-run China and establish her dominance over the Far East, the outlook for peace is such that only the most confirmed optimist can see anything but general war ahead.

The resignation of Anthony Eden as British foreign secretary may well be the end of a chapter in European diplomacy that sought to maintain collective action as against balances and blocs. With him goes the last vestige of whatever prestige remained with the League of Nations, and a return of power blocs ranged against other power blocs. It may be that this is nothing more than a return to realism, or the recognition of things as they are, but the thought is no less fearsome to western minds. Dictatorship is gradually extending its dominance, going from strength to more strength with every new coup, while the democracies struggle to maintain popular government against mounting odds, and the burden of taxation becomes heavier and heavier as the pace of the armaments race becomes ever swifter.

That Hitler and Mussolini, drunk with power, will long remain satisfied with present conquests is a forlorn hope. It is hardly a secret that Germany has an eye on Czechoslovakia. The Polish Corridor and Danzig are almost certainly on the list of future acquisitions. Hitler renounces territorial ambitions in France, but he gives no such assurance in the other direction. The initial step in the penetration of Austria has been taken. Where, indeed will he stop if not curbed and how far will he go before a curb is applied?

Idle questions and speculations, of course; but in the light of recent developments on the international scene, anything becomes possible – anything, that is, except the hope of a peaceful solution.

*   *   *

Twenty-five years ago – in the spring of 1913 it was – the Canadian government under Sir Robert Borden outfitted what was up to that time the largest and most thoroughly equipped scientific expedition ever launched, to study the Canadian Arctic, its life and conditions both on land and sea, flora, weather, etc., etc. Its staff of scientists, each a specialist in his line, was drawn from universities all over the world. Its commander was a native of Manitoba, V. Stefansson, who, though still in his early thirties, was already a distinguished scientist and scholar, an instructor in anthropology at Harvard. He had spent some time in the Arctic with the Mickelson-Leffingwell expedition, when he had adopted the Eskimo mode of life as to dress and eating and had learned their language, and had been a member of at least two other scientific expeditions of the National Geographic Society. The captain of the expedition's flagship, the Karluk, was Bob Bartlett, famed Arctic navigator who had served with Peary. No expense was spared to make this the most complete and best-equipped scientific expedition ever launched.

There seemed every reason to expect much from this venture in the way of knowledge wrested from the then little known north. Every effort had been made to guard against the unforeseen, and the commander himself maintained that accidents and adventures in such an undertaking should be laid first and always to inefficiency and lack of foresight. But he and others had failed to take sufficient account of the human element, which is often unpredictable, and which in this case largely nullified the success of the venture. That score and more of scientists was a body of eminent men; they knew much about hydrography, meteorology, etc., and were prepared to learn more. But one thing they had not learned, and were not willing to learn – discipline. What was even worse, they had pre-conceived notions about living in the Arctic, and these they would not yield, even when shown they were wrong. Stefansson and Bartlett tried valiantly to jettison these mischievous ideas and replace them from the store of their own experience, but these learned men could not be taught what was most important for them to learn. Why should they admit that an Eskimo, half-savage at best, knew better how to dress and eat and house himself and travel under Arctic conditions than they? Preposterous!

So when an off-shore wind blew the flagship with the ice-pack into the Beaufort Sea, with Bartlett and the main body of scientists aboard but the commander and Anderson, second-in-command, on shore, dissension and trouble arose. There could be but one end to that. With each man or group almost a law unto himself, disaster followed. The experienced Captain Bartlett and two of the crew eventually reached civilization, the rest perishing in their tracks, leaving their great learning – unkindly as it may seem to say this – with their bones. With all their knowledge they had not learned to obey or bow to greater experience.

For five years the commander and some of the members, not on the Karluk, carried on the work for which the expedition was launched, mapping the northern coastline, visiting numerous islands and discovering new ones, studying weather, flora, fauna on land and in the sea, sounding ocean depths, determining water currents, numbering and studying the Eskimos, etc., etc. Much of the knowledge gleaned in these years has been invaluable to those who came after and who are now making the Arctic a source of no little Canadian wealth.

In his epochal books on the work of this expedition, Stefansson gives no little credit to those who were not above learning – such as Hubert (now Sir Hubert) Wilkins, who has since made a name for himself in Arctic and Antarctic exploration, – Storkerson, Andreason and others. The difference lay in the closed and open minds – that of the scientists unwilling even to believe that sea water becomes potable on freezing (the salt being squeezed out in the ice) and so insisting on carrying fresh water with them; requiring "civilized" food and clothing, tents in place of snow houses – none of which answered to Arctic conditions nearly so well as those used by the Eskimos, and which were available everywhere. It cost most of the scientists their lives and the expedition much of its usefulness. But it at least afforded an object lesson in that all walks of life, be it exploration or stenography in a modern office, require discipline and the willingness to defer to greater knowledge and experience, without which no venture may wholly succeed.

*   *   *

Since the beginnings of recorded history the Jew has had a large place in the development of what we call civilization. From the country of the Nile, where he was for millenniums engaged in wars, his migrations can be traced in a crazy crisscross around the Mediterranean and through Europe, and later to the Americas. His wanderings began shortly after the opening of the Christian era, when the horrible campaigns of Vespasian and Titus (vide Josephus) in Palestine drove him forth after destroying Jerusalem and the Temple. From that day to this he has been a veritable "Wandering Jew" with no land to call his home, yet remaining essentially the Jew, unassimilable whatever his language or environment.

The victim of violence, oppression, persecution he has flourished and is to be found in most of the civilized countries today. Shrewd and calculating he has more than held his own in commerce against Gentile competition, who, when bested in the market or in the arts, has resorted to the weapon of numerical superiority and driven the Jew out on one pretext or another, confiscating his wealth in the process.

After 1000 A.D. the Jew began to flourish in southern Europe and, unwisely, to flaunt his wealth. This was one thing his Gentile competitor could not "take." So the Crusaders found a pretext to make Jewish wealth finance their campaigns, so "as they marched . . . they slaughtered Jews as they went." In 1290 the Jews were expelled from England; in 1394 from France. When the black death swept Europe in 1348 the Jew was massacred for it (his wealth always being confiscated in the process). But the Mohammedan Moors in Spain were tolerant, and here the Jew prospered. When the Christian Ferdinand conquered the Moors he ushered in a black day for the Jew, who, on a pretext of being a non-Christian became the object of persecution in what we know as the Spanish Inquisition, ostensibly a war on heresy, but actually a method of expelling the Jew minus his wealth. All throughout Europe he was legitimate prey. He was disbarred from holding land or joining guilds. So instead of becoming a farmer or artisan he became a merchant or middleman. Never knowing when he might have to flee, he kept his wealth in cash or negotiables.

From time to time the Gentile turns on him in savage hatred, killing him, driving him forth, and always managing to confiscate the bulk of his wealth in one way or another. Jew pogroms have at all times and in many lands of Europe and Asia been the order.

Today, beginning the second third of the 20th century, the plight of the Jew in Europe has in no whit lessened. In Germany, Poland and elsewhere his case is at once pitiable and terrible. Driven from one country he is spurned in another. Attempting to establish a homeland in barren Palestine he is set upon by the jealous Arab. Only in the Americas, notably in the U.S. and in England, is he in tolerable case, but this is scant comfort to the starving hordes in Central Europe where he is driven at the point of a bayonet to a boundary only to be met with refusal of entry.

It may be, as U.S. president Roosevelt mooted recently, that some world-wide movement will have to be launched to find the Jew a refuge, but at the moment humanitarian impulses get scant shrift, the energies of the world being more occupied with taking human life then saving it. In the meantime the Jew suffers, an alien and a stranger, whose plight is one of the black marks in the record book of western civilization.

*   *   *

This column is in the doldrums this week, its sails flapping idly, its foot deep in the Sargasso kelp. There is not even a gravitational pull in getting from up here to down there. Just a dead calm, the trade wind stilled; to the left the edge of Nothing, to the right mots filched from here, there and everywhere, followed by a warning of fire hazards. God's in His heaven, all's wrong with the world. Topping it all, it's "Firecracker Day," according to Bob and Brian, which is their way of observing the memory of good Queen Victoria, who had a way of saying, "We are not amused."

But we "see by the papers" as Will Rogers used to say, that another crisis in Europe has passed by without setting off the powder keg. The Czechs voted about something or other on Sunday and the voting was "significant" of something or other. And Hitler spoke at Munich without mentioning the Czech border incident, which also was considered significant, and the world breathed a sigh of relief and July wheat dropped three cents at Winnipeg. Not that any of this makes sense, Browning to the contrary, we insist that all's wrong with the world. Maybe the sun-spots are affecting us.

*   *   *

By all accounts there are a lot of people on this earth of ours – something like two thousand million all told, yellow, copper, white, black, in that order numerically. That's a lot of people, and they're increasing at a quite rapid rate. Our spinning globe being small, and it's surface about four-fifths water with an appreciable part of the land quite uninhabitable, we are told that habitable portions are becoming crowded. This is supposed to account for unrest in sections, such as Germany and Italy, where people haven't sufficient "elbow room." This despite the fact that you could pack the whole two billion of all the five continents and the thousands of islands into one box a half-mile square, with room to spare. They could all stand at the same time on the little island of Skye, off the Scottish coast, with lots of room to walk about. You could bury all the people of all the generations since Adam in a tiny corner of Manitoba. Yet they complain of being crowded and are quite ready to kill off their neighbors for more space around them, as Italy did in Ethiopia, as Japan is doing in China. Well, man is a funny animal, but not half so funny as he is vicious. No wonder the Lord repented that He had made him and tried to drown him in the rain-barrel. If man deserved it then, he probably deserves it in far greater measure today.

*   *   *

Papers and magazines, notably in the U.S., are making much of the fact that Their Majesties, King George and Queen Elizabeth, "are making a splendid job of their difficult task." This is particularly gratifying in view of the fact that due to the extreme feeling engendered by the abdication which brought them to the Throne, apprehension was voiced in some quarters as to their unqualified fitness. This has now been dissipated and the Crown and succession appear more secure than ever. In this connection it is interesting to note that Queen Elizabeth is the first British woman to sit beside a British king since James II married his Lord Chancellor's daughter in 1660. She is also the first commoner queen since then, although her father is Earl of

Strathmore and Kinghorne, Viscount Lyon and Baron Glamis, Tannydyce, Sidlaw, Strathdichtie, Bowes, Lunedale. Her parental home is Glamis (pronounced Gloms) Castle, "the oldest inhabited house in Britain," in which Macbeth is believed to have killed Duncan. Since her ascension the Queen is said to have "turned in a flawless performance," which is just about tops in praise.

*   *   *

This week the German government has massed a million trained soldiers under full equipment and on a wartime basis along the French and Czech borders. Belgium has 40,000 concentrated along the German frontier. The French-Italian border is closed to all traffic. War rages in Spain. Czechoslovakia expects invasion at any moment. In Great Britain air-raid shelters are being constructed and the entire population is drilling in gasmasks. – All Europe an armed camp, with peace to be likened to a man crossing the Niagara gorge on a tight-rope during a gale. A mad world, my masters!

*   *   *

Repercussions from last week's events in Europe are now asserting themselves. Following the ceding to Hitler of the rich Sudeten area of Czechoslovakia by Britain and France the full force of criticism of this abject surrender is now being heard. A bewildered world asks "why?" and echo repeats "why?" Hitler announced his intention of taking what he wanted of Czech territory, whose integrity was guaranteed by France and Russia, and in this the other great powers to all intents and purposes acquiesced. Chamberlain made three trips to Germany, ostensibly to persuade Hitler to modify his demands, the net result of which appear to be that France and Great Britain joined with Germany in demanding the partitioning of the richest industrial sections of the Czech republic between Germany, Poland and Hungary. Faced with this new front, the Czechs could do nothing but surrender, so in this sense it may be said that a pending war was averted and the "peace at any price" advocates appeased. At first this settlement was hailed by a world that doesn't want war, but as stated above, the repercussions are not all of one voice except in Germany, which was given all it demanded. A very important section of British opinion holds that Britain and France "sold out" to Hitler who goes from triumph to triumph, and that this peace at the expense of Czechoslovakia is but a truce, that eventually the Nazi-Fascist bloc, sometimes called the Rome-Berlin Axis, will challenge the democracies in a manner that even the "peace at any price" advocates cannot accept.

A disturbing voice is being heard – in Britain as well as in Winnipeg – to the effect that the "Cliveden Set," of which Chamberlain is the chief spokesman, is in reality pro-Nazi, in the sense that it fears Hitler and Mussolini less than it fears Russia and Communism. If this be only in part true, it explains some things not to be explained on any other grounds, including the ready dismemberment of Czechoslovakia, the apathy towards the Ethiopian and Spanish struggles, the retreat from sanctions, the abandonment of collective security, etc. This is the charge of Anthony Eden, Duff-Cooper, Winston Churchill, Lloyd George, Atlee, and an important section of the press. One can only hope that there is no truth in it; but the suspicion persists, and will not down.

*　　*　　*

Yippee and hurrah! This column has a reader, an honest-to-goodness flesh and blood reader down in far Ontario! Says it himself in a letter, believe it or not. "I have just finished reading 'The World at Large' in the Nov. 17 issue of *The Times* and felt that I could not let the opportunity pass of writing you and letting you know how much I enjoyed it. Might say that I read the article to the other two chaps who work with me and insisted that my good wife read it too. Keep up the good work and give us more stuff like it." Thanks. That makes three readers. Must be doing better.

1939

If dictatorship comes to us (and "it can happen here") in the western hemisphere, it will come mainly by reason of the inequality of income under our capitalistic system, and its corollary discontent. Today the top one percent in our income structure receives as much as the bottom 42 percent. That is inequality with a vengeance and makes one wonder whether any structure on such foundations can long endure. It can stand only so long as this bottom 42 percent is content to put up with it.

Democracy plus capitalism has its undoubted merits. Equally palpable are its demerits, suffered because we do not yet know what to do about them. With the profit motive dominant everywhere and in our smallest actions, this cannot well be otherwise. But from time to time the abuses under this system go beyond our tolerance, and we proceed to do something about some particular abuse or set of abuses, and not infrequently succeed in ameliorating or correcting them. We are now, for instance, considerably worked up about the deliberate "scamping" of manufactured articles, shoddy stuff made and marketed where superior and longer-lasting articles could be made at no greater cost, no more involved process of manufacture. It is charged that manufacturers deliberately shorten the life of their products to increase the volume of the sales. Electric light bulbs is a case in point. It is known that a slight change in the quality of the filament in an ordinary light bulb, involving no extra cost in manufacture, would treble its life, and necessarily decrease the volume of sales in that ratio. The switches for electric stoves is another example. These are so made that some small part in them, such as a few coil springs costing only a few cents, break, but the manufacturers refuse to sell parts, and the consumer is required to buy the whole switch at a cost of several dollars. So we continue to buy short-lived light bulbs and electric switches, to name only two, because the manufacturers desire a larger sales volume. This is one of the penalties of our competitive system, thanks to the profit motive underlying our every action, and the incurable selfishness of man in all his works.

*　　*　　*

There are two Englands, says Willem van Loon in a recent appraisal of Hitler and his chances of surviving for any length of time. One of them will destroy him, as it has destroyed some of his kind in the past. Hitler does not know history, and that defection will cost him dear. There are now and there have been for centuries two entirely different sorts of England, and so far Hitler is dealing with only one of them. "I am stressing this point," says van Loon, "for it is this often overlooked angle of the history of England which has led to the destruction of so many of her enemies during the last three centuries. Just when they thought they had that country in the bag, so to speak, they were forced to realize that they had only one part of it in the bag, and that the part that did not count most."

Do not judge England by Chamberlain, by the present or past governments or parties, or by any outstanding men or groups, says Loon in effect. The England that matters most is not particularly vocal, does not make its weight felt until its feeling are outraged, either from within or from without. But once aroused it is mighty, and almost invariably prevails. Hitler does not take this second England into account at all, judging it only by Chamberlain and that body of opinion for which he speaks – in power at this time but by no means in custody of the conscience of the people of England, which in the end will prevail. "Pitt tried to compromise with the revolutionary leaders of

France, but it was the conscience of Britain – that immovable minority when it comes to matters of truth and of inner conviction – which finally forced … the issue," and which in the end banished the heir to those revolutionary principles of which it disapproved to the lonely rock of St. Helena.

* * *

We live in a time of rapid changes. Being so close to it, our perspective is such that we cannot quite realize how terrific is the pace of these changes, which have transformed our mode of life more in half a century than in the previous nineteen. Since the turn of the century the motor car, the airplane, the radio – to name only three – have sprung like Juno upon a world not yet ready for them. The movies in this time have changed from a curious toy to a major preoccupation, and having reached the zenith of their development are admittedly on the way out, to be replaced by radio television. The prediction is that Hollywood and all that it stands for will pass within a decade, television providing all and more, at the twist of a dial, than is available in the cinema today. Thus does the world move, at increasing acceleration, man's technological progress outdistancing his mental and spiritual development until he stands bewildered before the work of his own hands, the Frankenstein that he creates in his ingenuity, momentarily threatening to turn on him and rend him. This is the penalty of too rapid progress. Man has left to grow up to his toys; he has not yet learned to ride the storm of his own making.

* * *

This week Pan-American Airways is inaugurating regular commercial service U.S.-England over the North Atlantic (via Newfoundland-Ireland) having already established the U.S.-France service via the Azores. Forty-two ton flying boats, larger than Columbus's caravels, ply both routes – giant four-motored ships, each requiring a crew of eleven with ample accommodations for 72 passengers. Thus far has aviation progressed in the 36 years since the Wright brothers' first flight in 1903, which lasted just thirty seconds. As an indication of the tremendous expansion pressure of the airplane production industry, each of the largest producers of planes in the U.S. – Lockheed, Boeing, Douglas – have backlogs (unfilled orders) of over $30,000,000, and these are only three of many.

SEPTEMBER 1939

Since the declaration of war by Great Britain and France against Germany on Sunday the one topic of conversation here has been the probable form hostilities will take and the more remote probable outcome. Not that anyone feels competent to foretell either of these, but speculation is in natural order. Battle is joined in declarations, but so far it is largely a war of words and propaganda, sound and fury but signifying much. The world of men is in for a trying and terrible time, the like of which it has never before experienced, unless some now unforeseen contingency intervenes.

At this time and from this distance it seems a vain hope to expect anything less than a long and bloody war of exhaustion, a contest which may outdo the wildest imagination of even a Wells, in which the side with the greater resources in men and materials as well as in patient doggedness will win a Pyrrhic victory. With the terrible engines of destruction now at the command of both belligerents, it will necessarily be sanguine and costly. If it runs a course of exhaustion, no one can now glimpse the state of the world at its termination.

Almost certainly it will be a long war. Germany will over-run Poland, consolidate her position on the east by cowing the smaller nations – Hungary, Rumania, Jugo-Slavia – before turning her attention to France and Great Britain. Then will ensue the battle of the giants, with Russia looking on from a distance, profiting by the weakening of the belligerents, whichever side wins. Whether the main theatre will be, as in the last war, in north-eastern France, or on the Italian plains leading through the Tyrol Mountains into Germany remains for time and circumstances to disclose.

But barring some new and unknown weapon at Germany's command (and so far there is no suggestion of this), Britain and France will win, whether the war be long or short. That is more than a pious and dutiful hope. They have greater resources, greater tenacity. Their people know they have right on their side, and that principles rather than profit underlie their actions. On the surface, this may not seem to count for much when guns are in action; but it does. In the long run it will prevail.

1940

Never in all the long years of recorded history has there occurred international defection to match the French reversal of policy at a time of grave crisis. An ally of Great Britain against a common enemy but a few weeks ago, solemnly pledged not to conclude a separate peace under any circumstances, the French government has not only broken that pledge by virtual surrender, but has assumed a definitely hostile attitude toward its former ally. Nor was this wholly brought about by France's military defeat and the armistice terms. Between the time that defeat of the armies in the field became a possibility or even after it had become a certainty, the government had ample time to dispose of the sea and air fleets and its huge supplies of gas and war materials in southern France to prevent these falling into German hands. Its failure to take steps to this effect can only be construed as a desire to strengthen German striking forces for the ultimate defeat of Great Britain, further borne out by subsequent developments and the set-up of the new French government headed by Marshall Petain, age 84, who is probably a "front" for the Laval clique. This government is now to all intents and purposes a totalitarian regime, in line with that of Hitler, Mussolini and Franco, and the principles of "Liberty, Equality, Fraternity," by which the life of the French nation has been ordered for the past hundred years, has now been put aside. That this is not in accord with the desire of the French people as a whole is assumed by British people here as elsewhere, who feel sorrow rather than anger at the French defection, and continue to cherish a feeling of friendliness toward the French people whatever its government may do. It is to be hoped that as the German heel bears down and the French people come to realize the full meaning and effects of German domination, they will also realize that the only hope of resurrection lies in British victory.

1941

We are being told to conserve energy and save materials in aid of the national war effort, even to forbearing to serve refreshments at social gatherings. This is not much to ask, and the Canadian people will readily fall in with this or any constructive suggestions designed to further the war effort. They will however, expect that the government and those in directive capacities lead the way in this as in other matters affecting public interest.

Early in the war this writer suggested to a member of parliament that the equipment, facilities and personnel of Trans Canada Airlines be turned over to the R.C.A.F for training of pilots. TCA had commenced operation only a few months prior to the outbreak of war, and as we had got along without airline service for a long time, we could do so again, now that a new emergency was upon us. The airline had a hundred or so first-class pilots, a score and more of new and expensive machines and as many first class fields, all admirably suited to the training of R.C.A.F pilots, mechanics, etc.

His suggestion went to the Dept. of National Defence for

Air, the minister, then the Hon. C. D. Howe, dealing with it in a public speech and his special assistant, Malcolm MacLean, in a lengthy letter. Said the minister in part. "I see no reason why Trans Canada Airlines should suspend or even curtail operations unless the war draws much closer to Canada. I see no merit in a proposal to suspend TCA services for the duration of the war and turn over the facilities to the R.C.A.F." Said his assistant, also in part: "It has been considered very desirable to retain TCA services at present as ... particularly valuable under certain circumstances, should the need arise for fast transportation of officers, or men, to any threatened part of this Dominion."

TCA flights later doubled and have now been tripled, with three daily round-trip flights Montreal-Vancouver. New fleets of the fastest airliners have been purchased in the U.S. (conversions of the Lockheed Hudson bomber) and personnel and equipment greatly expanded. During 1940 TCA planes flew over 5,000,000 ground miles.

This writer is still beset by doubts about the wisdom of continuing this service during this war. If there is need for conservation of material, skilled men and energy for the war effort, then surely this is a luxury the Canadian people can forego for the duration. The plea that an airline is needed to transport officers in probable emergencies is hardly tenable, since R.C.A.F planes could combine training with such flights when necessary, just as readily and just as efficiently as the airline's planes.

Flying 5,000,000 miles in a year with twin motored liners requires millions of gallons of gas and oil, over a hundred first-class pilots, thousands of skilled maintenance men, tens of millions of dollars worth of equipment, all of which could be used to good effect in our air-training program. Can we afford this expensive luxury at this time? Are the exhortations to the rest of us to cut down, even to "eats" at social gatherings, in good taste while the government maintains this luxury service for that section of our people who can afford to travel by air – the 55,000 passengers who used the airline last year?

Let's be consistent – turn TCA over to the R.C.A.F to further our war effort.

*   *   *

Announcement comes from Ottawa that the number of air-fields for the training of Air Force personnel is to be "nearly doubled" (91 are now in operation), construction to start at once. That this is a gigantic undertaking may be gauged by the fact that one of these new schools, construction of which is already underway – at Souris – is to cost two and a quarter million dollars. The 91 schools now operating are accommo-dating something over 80,000, and we feel safe in saying that not less than fifty as an average are being graduated every day of the week. To double this number of schools and their output is an index to the tremendous proportions of the war in the air to come, since there is already a large reserve of pilots and other personnel above present needs. In addition, training fields in the U.S. are available to R.A.F and R.C.A.F recruits, thousands al-ready undergoing training there. In view of this it may be said that the war in the air to come will be of proportions that only the liveliest of imaginations can grasp or even contemplate.

The Commonwealth Air Training Plan saw virtually all of the Allied pilots, excepting the Americans, receiving the majority of their training in Canada. The next item will also put that two-and-a-quarter million dollars into perspective.

*   *   *

Two new orders of the Dominion government this week have this column a bit cockeyed and jittery trying to reconcile them. One is the order to curb spending that more money may be made available for the war effort, and the other to institute mandatory wage bonuses to something like three million workers in industries, civil servants, railway employees, etc. Men earning up to $2100 a year will be paid bonuses corresponding to the increase in the cost of living, presumably to enable them to maintain the standard of living to which they have become accustomed. At the same time the cry is – from the government – that the general standard of living must be drastically reduced. Spending must be curbed, lest the demand for consumer goods promote inflation of prices. If these two orders are not contradictory we just don't know the meaning of the term.

1942

The manufacture of new passenger automobiles in the U.S. and Canada will cease when those now in process of finishing are completed; the sale of tires is banned, gas will soon be rationed; the sale of used cars is to be regulated; there is a suggestion that pleasure cars may be commandeered from those who do not need them urgently in their business. – The thought is finally boring its way through the adamant of our understanding that a lot of us are going to do without cars before this war is over.

*   *   *

The Canadian elector will shortly – on Monday, April 27 – be asked to mark a ballot "Yes" or "No" to the question of releasing the government from a pledge given on the manner by which men should be raised for overseas military service. This pledge was a plank in the platform on which the government appealed to the voters in the spring of 1940, towards the end of the "phoney war" period, when the outlook for the need of men deceived almost everybody, including the leaders of the Conservative and C.C.F. parties contesting the election, who gave like pledges. Much has happened since then, little of which was foreseen at the time, and circumstances have greatly altered. There is at this time no desperate need for the application of conscription for men to serve in the theaters of war, and such conscription may never be needed. Nonetheless, it would appear desirable to free the hands of the government for whatever measures it may deem imperative in the national interest, that the energies of the nation may be put to the fullest use in the war effort. It is for this reason that the electorate is asked to vote in this plebiscite. And the answer indicated is definitely "YES."

*   *   *

The country's voice on the conscription issue can hardly have been far out of line with what was generally expected in informed quarters. As a whole the people are for conscription, except for the fairly resounding "No" from Quebec. This throws the matter squarely into the lap of the government with a "here's your baby" implication, and this lusty baby is now scarcely less of a problem-child than before Monday's voting. It calls for no less courage today to put it in its place and make it behave, since the attitude of the people of Quebec has been brought into far sharper focus, and there never was any doubt how the rest of the country would vote. It is to be hoped now that the King government will assert its leadership without equivocation, since the returns can be construed only as an outright mandate in the matter, if sectional denials are properly ignored.

*   *   *

A quarter century ago there lived – and talked and wrote – a man at East Aurora, New York, by name Elbert Hubbard. (He and his gifted wife went down with the Lusitania). He was dynamic as well as a singular character, who no doubt made a considerable impress on the thinking of his time. The author of many books, he found time to edit two magazines while filling regularly up to 150 lecture engagements a year. While he will long be remembered for his "A Message to Garcia," which has sold in the millions, this writer chooses to remember him for a single remark he heard him make at a lecture in Winnipeg, and has stuck with him, in this wise: "The wish of the selfish to govern is often mistaken for a holy zeal in the cause of humanity." We have since come to believe that he might have added, that the first to translate the wish into the "holy zeal for humanity" are those who are already in the seat of government. They appear to fall, with fatal ease, into the belief that no one else can do the job they are doing with quite their own sure expertness, and that the country needs them, their experience and sagacity, as it needs nothing else. They are determined to save the country from the pow-wows which would surely follow their removal from office, and to yield to no entreaty short of booting, in this their "holy zeal." Let the sun go down and the cows come home, they will be true to their task and stay in office lest the country go to rack and ruin under another incumbent. 'Twas ever thus.

*　　*　　*

Emulating the quiz experts on the radio: – What act of a lady some ten years ago is now seen to have had a very important bearing on the course of the war? That's a tough one, as Clifton Fadiman might say, and would probably be "muffed" even by the experts on "Information, Please." Well, the answer is: the munificent gift of one hundred thousand pounds by the English woman, Lady Houston, to promote aeronautical research, primarily to build the air racer, Supermarine, which captured and held against all comers the world's airspeed record, and the coveted Schneider trophy, for the British. Out of this competition was developed the Spitfire, still the most efficient fighter aircraft, now credited with having turned back the Luftwaffe in

1940. The R.A.F received little official encouragement during the early thirties, and except for this assistance from Lady Houston it is quite conceivable that the Spitfire and Hurricane fighters would not have been the supremely efficient machines they were in 1940. Because they had the edge over anything Goering had to send against them, they prevented him getting air-supremacy over England and so very probably from invading the British Isles. Without the Spitfire, the direct descendant of the Supermarine financed by Lady Houston, the course of the war might well have been greatly, and tragically, different from what it has been to date.

* * *

A Saskatchewan small town publisher has a business card that is somewhat out of the ordinary. It reads: "George F. Baynton, Government Tax Collector." In small type down in the corner is this supplementary note: "Also – Editor and Proprietor of the *Lloydminster Times*." He has probably found that so much of his time goes to keeping tab of the Defence Tax, Income Tax, Sales Tax, Unemployment Insurance Tax, etc., that this is his principle occupation, relegating his work as publisher to second place. Others, including this writer, at times feel that way too.

* * *

Last week Canada welcomed officially the new Soviet minister. Representative press comment on this incident follows: "No diplomatic representation coming to Canada at this time would receive a warmer welcome than the Canadian people will give Feodor Gusev, the first minister from Soviet Russia ..." This is strange language from a press that outdid itself less than three years ago in reviling and damning the Soviet and all its ways. It was then the pariah among the nations of the world, denied diplomatic recognition, reviled and execrated in most of the world's major capitals. In 1940 the English language, here as elsewhere, was strained to its utmost in heaping abuse on the Soviet government and people. The Canadian press which now falls all over itself in a beaming welcome to the new Soviet minister took its full part in this abuse. Yet the Soviet government, the Soviet people and Soviet ideology have not noticeably changed in that time. The world has seen that the Soviet soldier can shoot straight and that he is prepared to defend his way of life; but is this sufficient cause for our about-face from execration to admiration of him? Surely not; but better late than not at all. It is merely that we have come to realize that we were wrong in our estimation of him and that we are now making amends as gracefully as we can. We now know that there was good reason for the Russo-Finnish war which had us so worked up that we all but frothed at the mouth in reviling the Soviet. The Russian people is now our ally, and a very worthy one, to which we extend not only aid but the hand of friendship. It is well in this case that our memory is short, else we might reflect with some mental discomfort that our attitude toward the Soviet was for a long time neither generous nor just.

1943

Add the cost of municipal and federal government and you'll begin to understand why you aren't rich. You'll probably begin to ask yourself if we aren't overgoverned. Might as well stop there, though, for all the good your questions will do. None of those governing bodies are going to vote themselves unnecessary. You've got them and you're going to have them until the cows come home, and that goes for not a few of the bureaus being set up in Ottawa.

But its all very impressive, and in a sense satisfying, however much you feel that there's an element of window dressing out front. Democratic government is like that.

*   *   *

Some things never change.

Announcement that Sarnia, Ont., is to be the nucleus of the important new industry of the manufacture of rubber in Canada affords further proof – if this were needed – that the West is "out of luck" in the matter of government assisted industries. The concentration of war industries in Ontario, Quebec and the Maritimes, with the almost sole exception of the D.I.L. plant at Transcona, has not passed unnoticed in the West.

*   *   *

CANADIAN-SOVIET FRIENDSHIP

Last week-end there convened in Toronto a congress which, for eminence in Canadian political, business, judicial, ecclesiastic, journalistic life, has not often, if ever, been equalled. In the "Call" to the press are given names of about 300 individuals comprising the council of this congress. This leads off with the Lieut. Governors of all our nine provinces, seven prime ministers, including the Rt. Hon. W. L. M. King, nine chief justices, senators, M.P.s, bishops, university presidents, top-ranking publishers and editors, generals, business and social leaders, and multimillionaires. Quite probably every important walk of our national life was represented on this council.

And what is the subject about which this galaxy of names ranges itself? To promote Canadian-Soviet friendship – no less! For three days eminent speakers enlarged on this subject, and committees busied themselves with matters and means of closer co-operation with the Soviet government and people, now and in the future.

Surely this is a laudable object and one worthy of support. It is not even startling, unless you look back – and then it does give you a bit of a jolt. Time was, and not so long ago at that, say

the winter of '39-'40, that it would have been difficult to visual-
ize such a gathering about such a purpose in Toronto's Royal
York. Soviet stock in Canada couldn't go any lower because it
was at the bottom, and individuals known to have said a good
word for it were in hiding or otherwise having a hard time of it.
It was only by the grace of good fortune, and the obstinacy of
Sweden, that the United Nations had not sent armies against
the Soviet in Finland. In case you wish to refresh your memory,
turn up a file of some reputable Canadian daily of that time for
a sample of what a man in the street was bid to think of the
Soviet government and all its work. In view of the gathering at
Toronto last weekend you might find it interesting.

Well, water still runs over the mill-dam, time passes and
Biddy's calf grows up to give milk. But our opinions and
prejudices follow no such order. They veer and slither and not
infrequently they get pushed around. Marching facts elbow
them in the ribs, slewing them around to new directions.

It has been so with our prejudices regarding the U.S.S.R.
The pariah among nations not so long ago, unworthy of diplomatic recognition, godless and terrible, which "socialized" its
women, enslaved its workers – this government and people are
now suddenly worthy. Our men of greatest eminence gather to
do them honor, and to devise means of closer ties of co-operation
and friendship.

Why this volte-face? Is it because the Soviet soldier can
shoot straight and to good effect? Is the Soviet so vastly different
today from what it was three-four years ago that we should now
change from revulsion to admiration and friendship? Questions
such as these jostle and insist on being heard.

The probable facts are that the U.S.S.R., government and
people, is today much as it was in the days when we reviled it. It
is our prejudices that have changed.

But that congress in Toronto last week-end is nonetheless
bewildering. It is one of those things that couldn't possibly happen, yet suddenly, and startlingly, it is there – "The Council of

Canadian-Soviet Friendship!" Well, it's all to the good. May it prosper!

*   *   *

LIQUOR RESTRICTIONS, AND RESULTS

Some two years ago the federal government intimated that it was going to regulate, and diminish, the consumption of liquor and beer by the public. Measures would be instituted making liquor less potent, much costlier and harder to get. Ergo: The liquor-consuming public would reduce their purchases and become more sober, industrious and law-abiding, as any well-regulated public should.

Some voices were heard at the time, including that of this journal, casting doubt that this desirable result would ensue. No end of previous "noble experiments" had not worked according to blue-prints of dry advocates, and there seemed little reason to suppose that this time it would be different. More people had more money to spend, on a narrowing market. More liquor and beer were being consumed, but not in alarming measure. It was suggested that this sleeping dog be let lie, and not alert either confirmed or casual drinkers to threats of impending shortage.

However, the government was determined to chase its ignis fatuus and began imposing restrictions. The first one brought prompt increases in purchases by the public, as has each succeeding restriction. Numbers of permit holders doubled, and evidences of stocking up by many increased alarmingly. The commodity, soon at a premium, was sought by many who had not previously bothered with it. Queues developed at liquor stores and evidences of black markets increased. Restrictions were not restricting.

As the vicious circle of decreasing stocks and increasing demand converges, matters not foreseen by the idealists, in and out of authority, develop. That could have been foreseen, with records of the dry twenties so available, but evidently one example in a generation is not sufficient.

The government now has the bull of prohibition by the tail, and from time to time gives it an added twist, and the critter is getting a bit restive. It is not a docile animal, and past efforts to get a ring in its nose have not been noticeably successful. Maybe it'll be different this time. Maybe; but we doubt it.

We are not above thinking that before the animal is properly stabled with a secure stanchion about its ample neck, both government and public will be thoroughly fed up with its cantankerousness. Let's hope that will not prove true; but from what we know of the nature of the beast (after watching its antics under the Saskatchewan Prohibition Act back in the early twenties) it takes a lot of taming.

1944
SOCIALISM – A SHUDDERY WORD

A word with sinister connotations to most people on this continent is the word "socialism." With many it conjures up specters of regimentation, "funny money," "what's yours is also mine" and other bogeys. The furor and universal shudders that swept over Canada as a result of some statements made recently by Harold Winch, a CCF spokesman, emphasized this phobia. The capital made of it by some old line politicians evidenced the general fear of the word.

What is there, after all and all, so terrifying about this word? True, it has had some unfortunate associations, notably that of Nazism and Fascism. Communism is also supposed to be an advanced form of socialism. Indeed, no end of scary things can be said of and about it. Until, that is, we recall that we have been applying practical socialism in many forms in Canada for a long time. Ownership vested in the people, with operation by the government for service without profit. What is our postal service, from the minister in Ottawa, to the rural carrier, other than applied socialism? What are our National Railways system, TCA, even the Bank of Canada, other than socialistic enterprises?

Then what is so terrifying about this word, when used by a Winch or a Coldwell? Is it because we have been told that it has obtained in Russia? It surely cannot be because our public schools are run on the principle of socialism – service without profit.

It may not be generally known that a sister dominion of the British Commonwealth – New Zealand – has been applying the principles of socialism to its everyday economy in considerable measure for a matter of over fifty years, and doing it without benefit of dictatorship – contended by many to be a necessary concomitant. Notably there are government housing schemes and medical services. The government has built tens of thousands of houses costing six to eight thousand dollars and rents them at three to five dollars a week. Anyone wishing to build a house for private ownership can borrow up to 90% of the cost from the government on very low amortized payments. Result – the average New Zealand home is very good indeed.

Medical and dental care are free to all. The government owns the hospitals and subsidizes the doctors. Result – N.Z. has the world's lowest death rate, including infant and maternal mortality, and the longest life expectancy, 65 years.

Old age pensions are automatic at 60 for women and 65 for men. Mothers' allowances are generous – about $29 a week for a widow with four children under 16. The overall objective of the N.Z. economy is security – that the individual may at all times be without fear of want, or becoming the object of grudging charity when his earning powers wane.

Socialism – a word to conjure up terrifying associations, with connotations sinister and shuddery. As a political bogey it is made to order almost ideal. It will be used often before the smoke of the next federal elections has cleared away.

Canada is not yet ready for any major socialistic experiments, such as common ownership of land, industries or the means of distribution of consumer goods. It won't be ready for some time, unless post-war readjustments are muddled beyond the breaking point of our collective patience. So whatever the complexion of our next government, whatever its platform, general socialism will not be invoked in Canada, by fiat or otherwise, within any foreseeable future.

So let's quit shuddering at the utterance of this sinister word. Socialism, generally applied, will come when the people as a whole are ready for it – not before – which will be, if ever, when capitalistic governments have messed up our national economy beyond endurance.

In the meantime we are applying socialistic measures, with fair success, in many forms. It is only when we forget that, that the word becomes frightening, sending the cold shivers up our collective back.

*   *   *

How some things do change.

Another sign, less compelling if by no means eclipsed, is the drive for funds to provide cigarettes for town and district boys serving overseas. The goal is a quarterly shipment of $150 worth, to eke out indifferent and costly supplies available to them in the foreign retail market and in service canteens. It may be argued that it is stretching the meaning of the word to classify cigarettes as a necessity; yet to a lad far from home, whether under the stress of battle, the long and hard grind of training or the loneliness of barrack life, smoking may be just that – a necessity. Such a life may be thought to be free and easy as seen from home or office under wartime economy, but it isn't. There is a strain to waiting as there is to action, and if we can do anything, provide anything, to ease that strain, we can do no less than "come through" quickly, generously, even gladly, adding our mite of thanks to those who take the initiative in this cause. So again – give to the Overseas Cigarette Fund – Now!

*   *   *

THE WORLD AT LARGE

(Standing subhead under above caption of a weekly column
in *The Times*, Treherne, Manitoba.)

My lords and ladies, let me state
Ere I upon my theme enlarge
Sum up the evidence, law relate,
And you, my freeborn jury, charge:
The accused is innocent of wrong
Till proven guilty -- lest the throng
With witnesses from near and far
Convict the prisoner at the bar --
That old rampageous reprobate,
THE WORLD AT LARGE.

(Attributed to Bogi with a degree of uncertainty.)

CHAPTER 3

MORALIST

Bogi Bjarnason was confirmed in the Lutheran Church at the age of thirteen, however, as an adult, he rarely attended church. His children say that as they set off each Sunday with their mother, Bogi would sit down and spread an old sweater across his knees preparatory to polishing his boots. Indeed, he only ventured into church for his childrens' school concerts and an occasional wedding or community event.

Yet, despite appearances to the contrary, Bogi had a deep religious faith. In his view, he didn't confuse the Church with religion. At best, Church was "an influence for the good." At worst it was a moribund institution which had failed in its duty as a moral leader. So while he often spoke of the Church with barely concealed contempt, he showed great respect and tolerance for other people's faith, whether Christian, Jew, or Muslim.

Bogi was undeniably fascinated by the Bible, which he considered a literary masterpiece. He believed that the stories in the Old Testament were worthy of both reverence and scholarly study, as they contained deliberations on the issues most crucial to humankind's understanding of the moral universe.

References to religion and biblical passages fill Bogi's writing. In editorials, essays, poems, and compositions, his faith is expressed in terms of morality and the human being's struggle between good and evil. He translated two of the Old Testament stories into verse. These stories, as well as a morality tale and other texts are included in this chapter.

THE PARSON'S DREAM

This piece appeared in the December 1926 edition of "The Golden Book." This prestigious monthly magazine was published during the 1920s and 1930s and featured short stories from some very well-known writers including W.S. Gilbert and Ralph Waldo Emerson. Unfortunately we let the large collection of them go to a used book dealer and now have only two copies, one of which contains this piece but lacks the cover. I remember going through the stack of them, reading randomly, and recall being impressed by the names of famous authors who shared the same magazine as my father.

*   *   *

The parson sat in his study whither he had retreated when his wife, spent with the day's work, had retired. For her the day had been arduous as were all Sundays, what with the entertainment of the usual train of callers and the supervision of meals, besides the work in the church, in which she took a good part. But if tired in body she was satisfied in spirit, and the pillow invited nature's blessed panacea.

Not so the parson. A vague uneasiness beset him. He had delivered two sermons as usual to practically the same congregation as upon this date the previous year. He had maintained his standard of merit in these sermons. The texts, he felt, had been appropriate, and the lesson logically built and thought out. Yet the fact was patent to him that his messages were for the greater part lost upon his flock. The parson was puzzled. More, he was annoyed.

Not that the feeling was new to him. The conviction had for some time been growing upon him that he was losing his hold. People were more apathetic than ever. They came, he felt, at the appointed hours every Sunday merely from force of habit and because that was the practice of respectable folk. He was not certain that some, at least, had not set out with wry faces, grudging it as a dismal duty, and sighing with relief at every singing of the Doxology. While dismissing the thought as unworthy, the parson could not absolve himself from blame in the matter, although the "age of materialism" (he was fond of the phrase) helped him out of every difficulty in this line. 'Twas a godless age!

He found comfort in this line of argument. For all that he and his brethren of the cloth did to exhort people to repentence, nothing availed. Once every week he ascended to Sinai to bring back some message from God, and each time he found his people at the feet of the calf of gold, whence nothing would move them. They would listen respectfully to his reading of the laws, then go back to the idol.

His annoyance abated as his thoughts went back to the last meeting of the vestry. Nothing could be finer than the manner in which the flock supported him and the church. They had advanced his salary unasked; all necessary changes were quickly and ungrudgingly made.

He played with the fire-tongs after relighting his pipe. His flock was satisfied with him and his work, had said so and showed tangible proof of it times without number. Thinking, his head sank upon his breast.

He slept.

*   *   *

THE
GOLDEN BOOK*
MAGAZINE

VOL. XI	CONTENTS for MARCH, 1930	No. 63

Published Monthly by THE REVIEW OF REVIEWS CORPORATION

DR. ALBERT SHAW, *President*   ALBERT SHAW, JR., *Secretary and Treasurer*
Editorial and Advertising Offices, 55 Fifth Avenue, New York, N. Y.

TERMS:—Monthly, 25 cents; $3.00 a year, two years $5.00, in the United States and Canada. Elsewhere, $4.00 a year. Entered at New York Post Office as second-class matter, December 6, 1924, under the Act of March 3, 1879. Printed in the United States of America. Subscribers may remit by post office or express money orders, or by bank checks, drafts, or registered letters. Money in letters is sent at sender's risk. Renew early, to avoid losing numbers. Bookdealers, Postmasters, and Newsdealers receive subscriptions.

EDWARD LANGER PRINTING CO., INC., JA'

He had left books and papers on the pulpit. How stupid of him. He must go at once and retrieve them.

Passing out of the manse he let himself into the church by the auditorium doors whence he had to traverse the main aisle. The mellow radiance of the moon broke through the stained-glass windows, painting saintly faces on pews and floor. An eerie feeling took hold on him. He felt Presences about him.

His foot encountered a limp something in the aisle. The parson was taken aback.

"Who and what art thou?"

There was no answer at first, save a muffled grunt as if coming from one who is being rudely awakened from sleep. He repeated the question. The creature crept under the pew, whence it made answer:

"I am Smith's religion. What would you with me at this hour? I am comfortable, and long to sleep undisturbed. Is it not enough that I do obeisance twice every Sabbath and at prayer meeting every Wednesday night?"

Smith's religion cuddled up and yawned. The carpet was soft and warm. Said the parson:

"Are you by chance alone here?"

"We are all of us here, Jones's religion and Mrs. Jones's and Brown's and Mrs. Brown's – and the rest. We are comfortable here. There is no place for us in modern life."

The parson reached under Brown's pew and brought forth his religious counterpart. It was a flabby, misshapen, potbellied semblance of that worthy citizen, Mr. Brown, broker. The parson shook it rudely.

The boneless legs wriggled, and the lustreless eyes rolled; its words were mumbled, unaccented.

"I am Mr. Brown's belief in God. The rest are here as well – his senses of duty and of shame, his conscience, his loves. We are fed on money, and kept here against harm. The diet is enervating and our bones are soft through lack of salt, lime and exercise. We are dying the death."

Mrs. Brown's religion broke in at this point. She was a thing of beauty, distinctly feminine, and gay in ribbons and bonnet. "My Easter hat, a perfect creation!"

She was at least sprightly, but lacked substance, whereas Mr. Brown's body was shapeless and all but lifeless matter.

The parson went from pew to pew, rousing the occupants with violent kicks and admonitions, fully determined to give them a wordy drubbing such as they had never before heard, for his ire was up. But when he had taken his place in the pulpit the entire congregation had sunk into their same deep sleep.

He awoke.

THE PRIEST'S INSPIRATION

(Based on an old Icelandic folk-tale)

The priest was a truly inspired writer of hymns. His verses had the quality of touching both singer and listener, so that no one who heard them was unaffected.

The bishop, a school mate and long-term friend of the priest, realized what a treasure his church possessed in this gifted man, and determined that his talent should not be tarnished by the accretion of habits and original sin. Among these habits, and the most conspicuous, was that he frequently drank immoderately; another, that he sucked snuff up his nostrils, not only excessively but uncouthly, so that it sifted upon the Cloth when he conducted services.

But that wasn't all, bad as it was. It was rumored that he was on intimate terms with a bright and lively young lady of the parish – more intimate than was thought seemly for a man of his standing. If this was not so much in evidence as his indulgence in liquor and tobacco, it thrived all the better for being passed around in whispers.

It thus came to the ears of the bishop. The gentry are ever privy to such intelligence. In this sense they are alike to the city, upon which all avenues converge.

The bishop consulted with the governor about appropriate rewards to the priest for his hymns. He consulted as well with the minister of health about measures to wean the priest from the bottle, the snuff and his lady-love, lest the church and his office suffer further thereby.

He agreed with the governor that the priest's talent should be recognized by the award of a Cross of Merit for his beneficent influence, a gold-headed cane to steady him on the slippery paths of life, a watch of gold to remind him of the passing of time, and lastly, a Bible, illuminated and gilded to draw upon for inspiration in further composition of hymns. The minister of health undertook to rid the priest of his obnoxious habits of indulgence in liquor and tobacco, but washed his hands in the matter of his light-of-love. The result was that the bishop took the girl into his own home as house servant. The health minister provided the "cure" for the priest's other habits by copious immersions in sulphur baths until the water ran murky and the patient emerged white and cleansed and minus his cravings, and bright and pure as a newly-minted coin.

The bishop approved of these developments, feeling that now his gifted underling would be lifted to new heights of accomplishment in the writing of hymns. But in the next three years not so much as a single verse was produced by the priest, now an exemplary man in all matters of public and private morals and conduct, strong in his condemnation of liquor and an advocate of abstinence from the degrading use of tobacco. He read his gilded Bible every day, carried his Cross of Merit conspicuously, swung his gold-headed cane and frequently consulted his golden watch about the passing of time.

At length the bishop wrote to the priest, asking the reason for his sterility in composing hymns – those beautiful lyrics that had so captivated the hearts of the people, lifting the spirit in paeans of praise to the Giver of all good. He requested the priest to send him a sample of his recent work of this nature, which must surely be of a high order of excellence to conform with his blameless life and high ideals, now that he had renounced his former ways and become a model of rectitude.

The priest responded with a number of verses in praise of

abstinence from liquor and ridicule of the use of snuff. "Good in their way," said the bishop enthusiastically, "but worthless as hymns."

"This damn thing won't do," he muttered upon reading the priest's verses. It was probably his first profane expletive in his life as a bishop. He was more than disappointed.

He summoned Mary, the serving girl, erst the priest's lady-love, first informing his wife to preclude possible misunderstanding on her part.

"You used to know the priest," he said to Mary. "You knew him quite well."

"Yes. my Lord Bishop, I guess you could say that."

"Did you, then, know the nature of his inspiration, the influence that prompted him to write his lovely hymns – those hymns so rich in praise of his Maker, so laden with acknowledgment of his own frailties and worthlessness?"

"Yes," replied Mary. "He used to compose them upon coming to after his bouts with Bacchus, in the throes of suffering and remorse. This was the mood that brought forth his most heartfelt and earnest pleas to his Maker for forgiveness, and strength to resist temptations."

"Is this all you know about it?" asked the bishop.

Mary resumed: "When well on the way to recovery after such sprees and able to resume his normal intake of snuff, he felt the peace of forgiveness surge through his frame. It was then that he composed his songs of thankfulness and praise."

"Very well," said the bishop. "This information may not be not wholly valueless. Do you then, perchance, know under what conditions he composed his hymns of adoration?"

Mary dropped her eyes and said nothing.

"So – so you don't know?"

"I prefer not to say," she replied, not raising her eyes.

"Did he, then, compose them when – that is, when, hum, when –?"

Mary looked up and replied: "Yes, he used to say that his

grandest periods of inspiration were when I was good to him. At least, that's what he said."

"Very well, does anyone but you know about this?"

"None but he – and you and I."

"Good, good! Keep it to yourself, my girl. There is no call for bruiting it about."

Shortly thereafter the priest received a sizable parcel. It contained a case of rum, and a store of choice snuff.

Later the bishop received a missive from the priest. It ended with: "Busy composing hymns as of old. *Magna est vis consuetudine*[1]. But they are not up to par in one particular. They lack the fire of adoration. Send Mary. *Pro Deo et ecclesia*[2]."

[1] Habit is strong.
[2] For God and church.

ALTERNATIVES

(From the Icelandic of Einar H. Kvaran. Translated by Bogi Bjarnason.)

The Soul lay wrapped in its long slumber, cradled in the ether.

Then the Lord had need of it, and He touched it with His scepter. It came out of the deeps of sleep in which it had dwelt from the beginning of time, and stood before the Lord – diffident, yet rejoicing, like the youth who has composed his first poem.

And the Lord dispatched it to the abode of men, where it would come forth in the shape of a child, destined to meet all the vicissitudes of life in the flesh, to the end of its allotted span.

After a time it came again before the Lord – terrified, as a hind after the chase; spent, as a lame bird.

"Dear Lord," it exclaimed, "the fear of this overcomes me. Grant, I pray, that I may return to sleep."

"What do you fear?" asked the Lord.

"I fear to enter upon human life. It is like unto a swollen river. I know not whither it may bear me. I fear that I may drown in its waters – its squalor, its ills of the flesh, its folly, its wickedness."

"You shall not drown," said the Lord. "I shall grant you some of life's greatest benefits."

"What will that be?" asked the soul.

"I shall make of you a man; I shall give you a woman who shall be very near and dear to you. Her very word shall be to you as a bar of a symphony; her every move shall, in your sight, be as laden with grace as undulations of grass before the wind; her very shortcomings shall be to you but fresh evidences of innocence. Asleep and awake she shall occupy your dreams."

But the soul pleaded that it might return to sleep. "Love dies," it replied. "I have seen that in the earth. Within a few years the mind will have turned to other things. Otherwise I were not man."

"Then," spake the Lord. "I shall fashion you into a woman. You shall mate with the man your heart desires. Your pleasure shall be to make him happy; to shed over him the effulgence of your love; to irrigate his heart; to bring light into his life so that shadow may nowhere darken it." The soul protested that it would rather sleep. "When his mind strays from me, I shall look after him with tears in my eyes and grief at the heart. Otherwise I were not woman. I have seen this, likewise, in the earth."

"You are difficult to please," said the Lord. "These alternatives are extended only to the elect of Fortune. Nevertheless, I shall hold out to you that which is better still – I shall give you Love and Good Will to All. It shall be your greatest desire to make mankind wiser and better. None so poor, so ignorant, so puffed with pride, so cruel, but that he shall have a part in your love. Your thoughts shall be of others, for others. You shall give them all that you have – your wealth, your food, your raiment, even to the peace of your mind."

"But will I also possess and enjoy the love of men?" asked the soul.

"No," replied the Lord. "That is asking too much. I am not sending you to paradise, but to the abode of men. And there – not even God Himself can persuade men to love him that loves them. The more that you love them, the more they will question your motives. You will appear to them to be either a knave or a fool. They will heap contumely upon you; the very cloak that hides your nakedness, every favorable word about you, every smile that may light your countenance – will become objects of question. If you escape crucifixion, you will have only their lack of manliness to thank. But your measure of good will toward men will enable you to bear it all with courage and fortitude."

"Let me rather sleep," pleaded the soul.

"You are particular," said the Lord, "These alternatives are held out to no one else."

And the Countenance of Mercy was cast down, for the Lord God knew that the Soul of Man desires not that which is most to be desired, and spurns it or ever it offers.

"One more choice," said the Lord. "I will give you dominion over men. Whether or not your words shall be of sense and virtue, they shall be charged with the spark that fires the minds of men; whithersoever you may wish to lead them, they shall follow you. They shall grovel before you, like worms in the dust. When, by your decree, they are flayed, the very lash shall become an object of veneration. You shall be an object of emulation to youth, and the dearest wish of every mother shall be that her son may find favor in your eyes, that you may not visit your wrath upon him. You shall be great and powerful in the eyes of all men."

Then the soul fell upon its face before the Lord, seized with joy and thankfulness. Without a word it arose and hastened on its way to the abode of men. The Lord looked upon its precipitate flight and sighed.

"It is like all the rest," He muttered. "It gave no indication as to what ends it would use its great power."

Anno MCMLX. No rights reserved ("including the Scandinavian") by the author, Bogi Bjarnason. First -- and last -- edition, six (6) copies, of which this is one. Set in Remington type.

THE "MARK OF CAIN"

A sinner's way is hard, 'tis said,
Rough, and steep, unstable.
Take Cain, a jealous type and bad,
Who slew his brother Abel.

In wrath the first to raise his hand,
And thus the first Grim Reaper.
Evasively then made demand:
"Am I my brother's keeper?"

The story, taken as a whole,
And whether fact or fable –
The Mark of Cain upon his soul,
Poor man, with scarlet label.

Engraved upon his brutish mind
With sin and sorrow weighted
Trudged forth, with Paradise behind,
To death addressed, and fated

For unremitting toil and tears,
To bear his load in sorrow,
Beset by doubts, by storms and fears,
To face a bleak tomorrow.

Rebuked, he hung his head in shame,
Filled with a nameless terror.
He felt the infamy of the name,
With error piled on error.

MORALIST

Eastward to the Land of Nod
His cheerless way he plodded,
Spurned by mankind, and by God,
And by his conscience prodded.

His punishment severe, condign –
Now questions came unbidden.
What the future? What, in fine,
Beyond his sight was hidden?

Questions crowding on his mind,
His guilt a gadfly stinging.
What before him? What behind?
His heart in anguish wringing.

Quick people all consanguine kith
(No Marilyn or Grable);
Whom would he cohabit with –
Sisters Beth or Mabel?

Were father, mother now the ones
To waylay and betray him?
And who was there to bear him sons?
Who was there to slay him?

Poor Cain, a wretched outcast then,
His sin a scarlet label. –
Poor Cain, despised of God and man,
Who slew his brother Abel.

– B.B. (August '56)

156

JOB — A COMEDY

PROLOGUE

The book of Job, one of the thirty-nine Old Testament books, relates a strange story – surely one of the strangest in all sacred literature. It tells of a district chieftain, an aga, a provincial princeling and a most successful agrarian, who becomes a "football," kicked about by the opposing forces of Good and Evil contending for the survival value within his frame. God and Satan, once master and servant in Zion, now (and since the rebellion there, so well described by Milton) chiefs of Heaven and Pandemonium, strive for his soul.

They meet at Job's stead in Uz, and after customary "small-talk" God challenges Satan to divert Job from his Godfearing ways – in modern parlance, he "sells him down the river." It is in effect a wager. "Do your damndest. Heap on him all the calamities, all the indignities you can manage: Job will not desert me." Poor Job, the victim, wavers. Beset by misfortunes from all sides, he doesn't understand, and he despairs – pleads to Death for extinction, for succor, to end his plight. Who of us can blame him? But this is his sin.

Out of the whirlwind God addresses Job, berating him in what is surely the least explicable of all recorded statements of divine origin. But eventually Job is restored to former well-being and affluence, with something over (though other victims of this "practical joke" remain dead). Let the reader find the moral. This scribe is unequal to it.

To orthodox Jewry (and some other faiths) things related in the book of Job took place precisely as set forth. To a scholar of another faith the story may be symbolical of the struggle of contending forces for the Soul of Man. In this the author is a bystander – a neutral.

In conformity with usage of the King James Version, pronouns are not capitalized.

COMEDY. – Webster: "Chiefly a term of literary history or criticism, applied sometimes to serious works whose purpose is to portray truth or life without leaving a painful or tragic impression, esp. 'The Divine Comedy' of Dante, and 'The Human Comedy' of Balzac."

– B.B.

JOB -- A COMEDY

Aga Job, a husbandman of worth,
Integrity, godfearing; in his prime
Amassed much earthly treasure, yet preserved
His pristine innocence and piety.
He was much favored by the Lord of Hosts
Who showered on him blessings and great store
Of mundane wealth and spiritual fare
Until he was "The greatest man of Uz."
His household vast and his farflung domain
Stretching beyond the eye on every hand,
His herds beyond compare:
    7000 sheep,
    3000 camels,
    500 yoke of oxen,
    500 she-asses;
The greatest of his treasures, seven sons
And daughters three, all godfearing and fine,

Whose wont it was to feast on natal days,
Always invoking blessing on the fare
And in like manner giving thanks to God --
Admonished by their father to observe
Decorum in their every phase of life.
Blessed then was Job, a happy man,
Nor had ill-fortune ever looked his way.

It was at one such festal gathering
Two uninvited guests looked on the scene,
Invisible, inaudible, save each to each:
God, the omnipotent, the king of kings,
And his erst vizier, Satan, lord of Dis,
Immortal chiefs of widely different realms.
The two conspirators stood on a knoll and talked
As would associates of old if haply met
By chance or otherwise upon a foreign strand,
Though now contenders for a certain prize --
The souls of all the progeny of Eve
Whom Satan had beguiled with "applesauce"
To bring corruption to the world of men.
The twain now stood upon a knoll in Uz
Above the stead of Job and, side by side,
Surveyed Creation's wonders and the work
Of Man in bringing order to the world --
Stood companionably and at ease
And sans hostility or enmity.

Said God to Satan, in effect, "What now?
How are things with you? How do you fulfill
The passing moment's stern demands to earn
Emoluments to balance need and pride?"
Then answered Satan:
"From going to and fro in the earth,
And from walking up and down in it."

Then saith the Lord, "Seest thou my servant Job,
An upright man and just, eschewing sin
And prospers greatly in due consequence?"
Said Satan: "Doth Job fear God for nought?
Dost thou not hedge about him and about,
Blessing his handiwork on every side,
Increase his substance, magnify his flock?
But now put forth thine hand and halt his weal,
All that he hath; make contrary the wind
To blast his flocks -- he'll curse thee to thy face."
Answered then the Lord: "All that he hath
Be in thy hands to do with as thou wilt
Save in his person; his body must thou leave
Inviolate, and in no manner harm."

In such words did God deliver Job
Into the hands of Satan to despoil,
Tempt, make sport of and defile.

They parted then -- Satan to his task
Of bringing dire catastrophies to Job,
The unwitting victim of this cruel sport.
Now rained calamities upon his head,
In swift succession devastating all
His worldly treasures, but not yet his faith.
A wind from out the wilderness laid low
The house where sat his progeny at meat
Killing all ten; fire from heaven consumed
Servants and sheep, while hostile, harrying tribes,
Sabeans, Chaldeans raided, carrying off
Camels, asses, smiting hip and thigh
His loyal servant force, til all was lost.
Now rent poor Job his mantle, shaved his head,
Yet fell upon the ground and worshipped God:

"Naked came I out of my mother's womb,
And naked shall I return thither;
The Lord giveth and the Lord hath taken away;
Blessed be the name of the Lord."

*   *   *

And yet again the Lord and Satan met
Upon the selfsame knoll to further scan
The work of evil wrought upon poor Job,
Who in the degradation of his straits
Was now reduced to penury and shame.
Said God to Satan: "Seest thou my servant Job,
My faithful servant, staunch in weal and woe,
Immune to blandishments, nor yet deflects
From true integrity, a just and upright man?"
Then up spake Satan: "Put forth now thy hand
And touch his flesh -- he'll curse thee to thy face."
Then saith the Lord: "Lo, he is in thy hands.
Sear his flesh, but do not take his life."

Now was poor Job fell stricken in his flesh,
A mass of suppurating sores, sole to crown
Which he scraped with a potsherd where he sat
Among the ashes, while his loving wife
Rebuked him in harsh words -- "Curse God and die!"

Then came three "comforters" upon the scene
To bear him company in his distress --
Came and wept and sat in silent grief
Nor any spake for seven days and nights
Of contemplation of his utter woe.

Then opened Job his mouth and cursed his time:
"Let the day perish wherein I was born!

Would that I had, a puking infant, died."
In many words did Job berate the day
That brought him forth from out his mother's womb,
The breasts that nurtured him, the spark of life
Within his infant frame that kept its hold.
"Would I had died, been gathered to the bourn
Where prince and pauper lie, and troubles cease."

Then up spake Eliphaz, one of the three
Come to bring comfort, saying, in effect:
Your sins have tracked you down, have found you out,
For they who plow iniquity, sow wickedness,
They reap the same, by blasts of God consumed.
Afflictions cometh not forth of the dust,
Neither doth trouble spring from out the ground.
Lo, happy is the man whom God corrects,
So must not thou despise this chastening,
For knoweth this, that man is born to strife
Even as the smith's bright sparks fly up.

Then answered Job and said, Lo, I am faint,
My burden heavier than I can bear.
For one thing do I long, That I may die,
But this too is denied, and I despair.
Now would I die, be as a cloud dispelled,
Vanish away, and go down to the grave
Never to return. I would not live alway.

Bildad, the second of the comforters,
Now spoke his piece, in substance both rebuke
And promise of redress when punishment
Wipe transgression from the slate of life.
"Doth God pervert judgment?
Or doth the Almighty pervert justice?"
Thus were Job's suppurating mental sores

Rubbed salt by accusation that his sins
Were being expiated by his suffering,
His heavy fardels compensating weights
To balance guilt, the errors of his past.

Then answered Job in tones disconsolate:
"Shall man contend with God, which made Arcturus,
Orion, Pleiades, the chambers of the south,
Great things past finding out? Then who am I
To reason with his might? Though I were righteous
I would not answer -- merely supplicate.
Yet must I speak of life that is too harsh,
Expostulate with God that I must bear
Afflictions that my soul can scarce endure.
So shall my bitterest complaint be on myself,
For I am made of clay, his handiwork,
A creature of his whims, and now condemned.
His hands have made me and have fashioned me
Together round about; yet am I imperfect,
My sins incarnadine of hue and of a count
Beyond all computation. Woe is me!"
Such in substance was the plaint of Job.

Now Zophar, last of his three friends
To raise his voice in admonishment
Berated Job for foolish talk and vain
To this effect, in accents harsh and blunt;
Know, Job, that God exacteth of thee less
Than thine iniquity deserves. Now think!
Canst thou by searching find and measure God?
But now prepare thine heart, stretch out thine hand,
Depart from wickedness; so shalt thou be
Rewarded in full measure and the day
Of thy redemption dawn. Be of good cheer.

Then Job in pique if not in anger spoke:
"Wisdom will surely die with you, my friends.
But I have understanding too, not less than you.
Now am I mocked in my affliction, rent
In soul and body by my comforters.
The just and upright man is laughed to scorn.
Robbers prosper and the evil brood
Thrive in security; into their keep
God spreads abundance with a lavish hand."
His wonted patience ebbing in his plight
He now erupted in a verbal spray,
Laying about with words pejorative,
Heaping invective on his triple friends,
But reasoned high in thoughts most elevate
About the Lord's unquestionable might,
Foreknowledge, fate, fixed fate of world and men
Til, lost in contradictions and the maze
Of squaring knowledge absolute and will --
Free will -- with all that's foreordained
Full circle meets and all acropper lies.

Now question follows question in a spate
Of observations on the guilt of men
In correlation to the will of God --
Almighty God, creator of the world,
His essence, attributes and origin.
Now was poor Job bemused, set all adrift
Upon a sea of contradictive swells
That rocked his skiff of reasoning about
And set it yawing in erratic tacks,
From harsh invective on his whilom friends
And deeper cogitation on the Lord.
Descanting in apt epigrams and terse
Upon his own transgressions and the guilt
He owned to, Job yet blamed stern fate,

Events inevitable to the creature man
By sin corruptible and to death addressed.

Man that is born of a woman is of few days
and full of trouble. He cometh forth like a
flower and is cut down; he fleeth also as a
shadow and continueth not. ... Man dieth and
wasteth away; yea, man giveth up the ghost, and
where is he? ... Man lieth down, and riseth
not; till the heavens be no more, he shall not
wake, nor be raised out of his sleep.†

Eliphiz, in terms of reprimand
Now charges Job with lack of piety;
He proveth that unquietness in men
Is due to folly and to wickedness.
To which Job answered with a meet reproach
Of carping "friends" whose sympathy was strained,
Unfeeling of his case, *sans* pity of his state
And arrogant contumely and pride.
Now waxed the wordy conflict of the four
Inveighing one against the other till,
With tempers ruffled, barbed and hurtful words
Passed to and fro like arrows shot from bows
In mortal tilt when adversaries meet.

Job's hope now centred not in life but death,
Sweet death, to bring him succor and redress,
Till Bildad interjected his reproof
Of such presumption and impatience,
Citing that calamities will hound
The wicked, proud, and the unworthy man.

†*All marked paragraphs were not of Father's composing, but were taken straight from the Bible.*

Thus Job beseeching pity on his plight
Was met with accusations and reproach
Yet sought to maintain countenance and pride
Despite abandonment by God and man.
A backward look toward his former state
Of well-being and worldly affluence
Brought anguish to his sad and rheumy eyes
As inwardly two pictures came in view
Of former glory and present misery.

And now another recruit to the force
About him came upon the scene -- bland Elihu --
Whose counsel, sage and weighty, bore upon
(In dissertation lofty in content)
The majesty and greatness of the Lord
Whose ways inscrutable are far beyond
The short and feeble intellect of man
He sheweth clearly that the puissant Lord
Is by the very nature of his work
Exempt from justifying what to men
Appears irrelevant, or not within their ken
Or understanding. God is ever just --
Cannot be otherwise -- and therefore Job
By his afflictions is expiating
The errors of his ways and load of guilt.

Now there descended from the vault of heav'n
A wind that whirled and spiralled awesomely,
From which a voice issued, imperious,
(And in its timbre, majesty, and might),
Directed to the "comforters" of Job,
Bildad, Zophar, Eliphaz, laying the whip of scorn
Upon their naked, vulnerable backs
For errant ill-conceived and carried out

Yet worse, in bringing balm to Job.
The voice judicial berated all the three,
Assessing fines; seven bullocks, seven rams
For a burnt offering in the sight of Job.
This carried out the three and Elihu
Were then dismissed and sent upon their ways.
The voice then turned to Job in accents stern
Accusing him of folly and the sin
Of self-appraisement and obnoxious means
To ward off blows aimed at him by his friends,
The wordy gusts in substance tersely thus
(Here freely paraphrased and rendered down,
The gist nowise departing from the text
Save in omitting sundry lesser jibes,
Nor adding arguement for seasoning):
Who art thou to talk? And where wert thou
When I conceived and shaped the universe,
Laid the foundation for the vault of sky?

Who is this that darkeneth counsel by words
without knowledge? Gird up now thy loins like
a man; for I will demand of thee, and answer
thou me. ... Hast thou commanded the morning
since thy days; and caused the dayspring to
know his place?†

Thou wert not yet born when I devised
And formed the keystone of the firmament,
Set the limits where the waters meet
The solid crust and there cause to be flung
Back upon itself in angry spate
Of breakers at the feet of tow'ring cliffs;
When I created stately behemoth
Chief of (all) the ways of God on earth,

And ponderous leviathin that breasts
The ocean sea with phosphorescent wake,
Breathing fire while the waters boil.

Thou, Job, sanst not create such wondrous things
Nor canst thou tame the unicorn, command
The rain to fall, the snow to know his place.
Thou dost not feed the ravens, nor yet sate
The hunger of the lion-young who cry
To God in their extremity for meat.

Thus God berated Job in many words,
Heaping hot coals of scorn upon his head
Now drooping under charges of much guilt --
Of talking out of turn, and of his lack
Of due humility for shortcomings:
Inability to guide the stars aloft,
Not knowing where the darkness hid by day,
Not being born when earth and firmament
Came into being at creation's dawn.

*   *   *

Now God relented and presumably
Withdrew what he had granted Satan -- right
To harass Job and make his life a farce
Of grim, exquisite torment well designed
To break his spirit and seduce his faith.
But faithful Job, unlike his ancestor,
Had withstood all the fiend's blandishments,
Had yielded only to despair, forspent,
And prayed to Death for succor from his plight.
That was his grievous sin, which God forgave,
Restoring him to health and affluence
And former state of honor in the land.

His flocks now numbered:
    14,000 sheep
    6,000 camels
    1,000 yoke of oxen
    1,000 she-asses
Fairweather friends now crowded to his board,
The foremost those who in his dire distress
Had passed the other side nor looked his way,
Alike the priest and Levite of the tale
When Good Samaritan "picked up the tab."

After that lived Job for happy years
Twice seventy in full favor of the Lord,
Gat seven other sons and daughters three,
Replacements of those cruelly deprived
Of life in youth, with all the servitors
Swept off the scene as so much worthless clay
Sans right of joyment and in the midst of life.

        *   *   *

So endeth here the Comedy of Job,
A creature-sport of dual principles,
Life and Death contending for the spark
Of what survival value there remained
Within the limits of his corporal frame.
But what the moral is escapes this scribe,
His intellect unequal to the task
Of winnowing the kernal from the chaff
And garnering the cereal nutriment
Inherent in the tale so ably told.

He stacks his flailing instrument and leans,
Bemused and hesitant in silent gaze,
A solitary gleaner in the field

Of wisdom where the harvest, overlush,
Defies his efforts as a laborer
And husbandman to sack, and store, and keep.
A westering sun squashed on the rim of night
Suggests a period and taking final leave
Of Job restored to his former state,
After the turmoil of his grim descent
Into Avernus, and the bleak despair
Of utter hopelessness -- now back
To Eden takes his swift, triumphant way.

EPILOGUE

The very scholarly analysis of the story of Job in the *Encyclopedia Britannica* suggests that it was reduced to writing in the 4th century, B.C., having probably existed in oral form for a long time and passed on, generation to generation, with changes and accretions. It is definitely the work of more than one writer, style and wording (in the King James version) differing materially one section from another, with evident later interpolations. The fanciful allusions to animals -- the fire-breathing whale (leviathan), hippopotamus (behemoth) and unicorn in chapters 40 and 41 -- are assumed to be from a later date.

Bibliography is extensive. The story of Job has probably had more books written about it than any other O.T. book, evidence that many thinkers have been intrigued by it and sought for the meaning and message. But as "the proper study of mankind is man," so is the proper study of it the book itself rather than books about it. It is a gem of literature, worthy of the utmost attention and scrutiny, as well as reverence, that the serious scholar can bring to it.

NOAH AND THE FLOOD

Condensed from The Word of God,
Chapters 6-9 Genesis

Noah, grandson of Methuselah,
A man of stature and integrity
Who "walked with God" and in his daily life
Kept his commandments and forebore to sin
As did the rest of humankind extant
(Save in his cups, when he was prone to err),
Was now selected by the Lord of Hosts
To play a part in rectifying wrongs
Committed by the Lord himself. His kind
Was to be wiped from off the face of earth
Together with all other forms of life
(Save only fish) in devastating floods.

The Lord had erred in making creature man
In His own image, breathing pulsing life
Into the dust, man's basic element,
Unfit to cope with master Satan's guile.
God the omnipotent, all-knowing, just,
Had erred, and now repented of His deed;
Man in His image was a failure -- worse,
His essence evil, and unfit to grace

God's footstool and continue in the way
He heretofore had chosen to pursue.
Now must he be destroyed, erased, *en masse*
Together with all other living things,
Flesh and fowl and every creeping form
Save only Noah and his progeny
In one spectacular catastrophe.
The Lord apprised good Noah of His plan,
Instructing him to take the vital steps
For preservation of himself and kin.
The means -- construct an Ark three storeys high
Of vast dimensions --

And this is the fashion which thou shalt make it of:
The length of the Ark shall be three hundred cubits,
And the height of it thirty cubits.
A window shalt thou make in the Ark,
And in a cubit shalt thou finish it above,
And the door of the Ark shalt thou set in side thereof:
With lower, second and third storeys shalt thou make it.†

As ordered. he built the Ark of gopherwood,
In seven days of labor, pitching it in and out,
Provisioned it with food and fodder, enough for all,
Vegetarian and carnivori, their tens of thousands,
For a space of days ten tens plus fifty*
They would remain within the Ark. In short,
Sustenance for that length of time, and air
Provided by that single opening --

---

* Two accounts of the time spent in the Ark do not agree. Gen 8-3 gives the time as 150 days, Gen 8-5 says nine months elapsed before the tops of the mountains were first seen. Take your choice.

(It may be assumed that on the 150th day
of confinement the air in the Ark was rank,
for neither mammoth nor cicada was
housebroken. Little wonder that poor
Noah, far gone, on getting out got drunk.
But that's another story.)

Opened now the taps of heav'n above,
Pouring water forty days and nights
Inundating all known lands to depths
Of fifteen cubits (three plus twenty feet),**
Which made invisible the highest peaks
But bore up Noah's Ark with all it's load.
Happily the Ark had shallow draft,
Being but five plus forty feet in height --
(Half its width, and disproportionate)
Keelson to topmost deck, three storeys up.

When the Ark came to rest on Ararat
Noah took steps to ferret out the lay,
Sending forth a raven and a dove
Which told him how conditions were abroad.

Emerging, with all other life aboard
He built an alter to sacrifice
Unto The Lord, "clean" beasts and fowl in twos,
Providing such "sweet savor" it pleased The Lord
Who now blessed Noah and his progeny,
Bidding them breed
Replenishing the earth.

** Genesis 7, verse 20. The mount Ararat, where the Art came to rest, has
grown in height somewhat since that far day. The encyclopedia gives the
height of Ararat as nearly 17,000 feet.

The waters now "assuaged," dry land appeared
And Noah soon became a husbandman,
Planting a vineyard, the potent fruits of which
Laid him low in sleep within his tent.
Undraped as on the day that he was born.

Son Ham now came upon him thus, and shocked
Imparted to his brethren Japheth, Shem,
This disastrous news, that he had inadvertently
Beheld their father in his nakedness.
These two then took appropriate steps and prompt
Steps backward into the tent where lay their sire,
A quilt across their backs which they let fall
Upon him, and were thus spared the sight,
And spared the penalty.
When Noah woke he knew what Ham had seen,
Knew and was enraged, an awful anger
In which he cursed his younger son, poor Ham,
And all his progeny forevermore, henceforth
Mere servants to the rest of humankind.

(Genesis 9-25, 29: And he (Noah) said "Cursed be Canaan
(Ham); A servant of servants shall he be unto his brethren.
Blessed shall be … Shem, and Ham shall be his servant. God
shall enlarge Japheth, and Canaan (Ham) shall be his servant." –
And Noah after the flood lived three hundred and fifty years.
And all the days of his life were nine hundred and fifty years,
and he died.)

WHO DISCOVERED ALCOHOL?

Spiritus frumenti – grain alcohol in its various forms, has been on the scene for a long time and had its part in the shaping of history.

There is no direct evidence that Cain and Abel had it (though they might well have, since both were farmers), but certainly Noah, not long after them, had it and on occasion indulged immoderately, getting pie-eyed to the great and lasting detriment of Ham, one of his three sons, who happened to come upon the old geezer asleep and stark naked in his tent. Accident or not, that was something not to be suffered, as his two other sons knew and who took appropriate steps – backwards with a blanket over their shoulders which they then let fall. There is a song setting forth that Noah upon emerging from the ark went on a bender (who can blame him being cooped up with all those animals for nigh on a year with only a 2' x 2' vent for air). And who knows but what Elisha was a bit high when he cursed the children and summoned a she-bear from the forest to tear 40 of them for calling him a baldpate.

The first miracle Jesus of Nazareth performed was to turn water into wine to enliven a wedding feast. And before that, quite likely Paris and Helen said "bottoms up" before eloping to Troy.

Then the knights of the Round Table. No doubt they had their moments; for who would say, "My strength is as the strength of ten because my heart is pure," without an ounce or two under his belt? Reminds you of the mouse in the barroom that had lapped up some spilled stuff before declaiming: "Now where is that cat that was looking for me yesterday?"

Next there was Mohammad the prophet who banned whatever it was his converts drank. He made it stick, too, for to this day no true Moslem takes a drink. And just think of the benefits! They know what-all about the Koran, and some have even learned to read.

A couple of hundred years after Mohammed the Scandiwegians took to mead and piracy, raising Ned in the Western Isles, including England and Ireland. They got to be such a pest that even King Alfred was obliged to hide out, and in the process allowed the old lady's cakes to burn. Really, the evils of strong drink are beyond compare.

But in ten hundred-something Omar the Tentmaker sang its praises: "I often wonder what the vintners buy one half so precious as the stuff they sell." And on and on – Villon and King Hal, real tosspots; and Pepys and Schubert and Lamb and Shelley and Dequincy who sobered occasionally to write and compose deathless songs and prose. And General Grant. Said Lincoln: "Send him a barrel of the stuff, if thereby he wins battles and shortens the war."

It seems that there has always been liquor, and that its effects have shaped events to no small extent. From the beginning of agriculture pigmash has produced alcohol and men have sampled it.

But only recently were its real potentialities discovered and exploited. That momentous event fell to a Canadian provincial premier in the mid-twenties of our century. Liquor had been outlawed in much of Canada during WWI, and in the U.S. a Minnesota senator by the name Volstead had got a bill enacted banning manufacture, sale and consumption of it in any form in his country, thereby launching Capone, et al, in Chicago and incidentally some large-scale liquor interests in Canada, notably Saskatchewan. The prairie provinces were dry at the time – dry in the sense that the Florida Everglades are dry. "Temperance Acts" were on the statute books and all was well.

On a day in the early twenties this writer attended a hockey game in a smallish Saskatchewan city and put up at one of the hotels owned by the aforementioned liquor interests. This hotel was also the headquarters of the local detachment of the RCMP, whose officers roamed the countryside looking for pigmash that had started working. Where this was found – not infrequently – the unlucky farmer would part with $200.00 or go to jail. But this night of the hockey game you could buy a bottle or a drink-by-the-glass at this hotel, delivered by obsequious Japanese servants, no questions asked. Of such nature was the alcoholic drought in the prairie provinces in the years following the first world war.

What hurt then was not just the flood of illicit liquor available to anyone who had the price, but the idiotic show of force to halt it; striking anywhere but at the source. Everybody knew where it was except the authorities told off to contain it, and whose concern appeared to center on pigmash at remote farms, mash that might, given the time to ferment, turn to alcohol and a $200.00 fine before a local J.P. That was grist for the judicial mill but scarcely a finger in the dam that showed signs of breaking. Illicit liquor was $8.00 the bottle ("How many do you want?")

The good old days!

*   *   *

Then on a day in the mid-twenties a plebiscite in one of the prairie provinces returned liquor to legal status. The legislative assembly called together to deal with the matter decided to make the vending a monopoly of the government. The premier (as related to this writer) looked down the long table and at his colleagues, his silent ministers, and then at the far wall, a gleam in his eyes. A terrific idea had hit him. He had just discovered alcohol – for the purposes of taxing. If Noah, and some others from his day to this, wanted it, so did some voters. So let them have it – at a price. Charge pu-lenty! The higher the price, the more people will want it. Boy, this is a gold mine, the mother lode. In that instant was alcohol discovered – as a producer of revenue. Noah, who on occasion imbibed and then cursed his son (but lived to be 950) didn't know its potentialities. We do.

So thanks to the inspiration of a provincial premier who looked at the ranks of his lieutenants and then at the far wall, lost in thought, alcohol was discovered. It's with us to this day, and will be till Gabriel blows. Said this premier, still in the ecstasy of discovery, "Let's go to town on this; appoint C. (a former and discredited cabinet minister) to manage the trade, at twice his previous cabinet indemnity, and make alcohol available to all who want it and have the wherewithal. A certain brand of whiskey brewed in Scotland from Canadian grain costs 90 cents the imperial gal. at its source; our price to the ultimate consumer, $36.00. Boy, what a bonanza! Eureka! Cheers and cheers! Now everybody will want alcohol, in all its forms – and our coffers will fill."

That wasn't the end of the matter. Other ways of enhancing profits from the sale of alcohol were devised and amended as other provincial governments took up the racket. At least one government outlet reduced the imperial quart of 40 oz. to a "re-puted" 26, then poured out a fifth of the contents and replaced it with water. Now double the price, and for good measure add a 5% sales tax. Man, this is really something! The well-to-do buy it no matter what. The old-age pensioners who might want the odd nip but can't afford it are better off without it anyway.

Thus was alcohol discovered, and the financial problems of Canadian provinces solved, once and for all. World without end.

MY PAL

We met that first time in a mirror facing a snack-bar on Hastings St., Vancouver, B. C. – the old saloon-days type of mirror, wide and clear. Shoulder-to-shoulder on stools we had not spoken, but his reflected glance was a friendly "Hi Pal," which I reciprocated. We then fell to conversing, with the result that he insisted on paying for both snacks, in the process displaying a roll of bills "fit to choke a cow." I was impressed.

In days and weeks following we met frequently, he on his rounds as a salesman of sorts (I was not to learn till much later what it was he peddled). Like myself a bachelor, we met often at nearby restaurants, and in time took to looking in at each others' digs, affably and unceremoniously. Having much in common we "hit it off" in the friendliest fashion. It appeared to me that he supplied something I much needed, the intimacy of a fellow-human, for at times I was lonesome. When he leaned an elbow on my shoulder and spoke into my ear, almost conspiratorially, I felt the "lift" of belonging. He was of that kind.

Yet he puzzled me; I couldn't quite make him out. Well off and carefree, dressing expensively and in style, if not always in the best of taste, he was an agreeable companion. That my girl Mary did not approve of him, even to the extent of "either he or I," was not enough to break my bond with him. His apartment was usually in a mess of disorder, the bed unmade, his clothes strewn about on the floor. That was just his way, and he made no excuses for it. Take it or leave it. Who cares!

*   *   *

I had a job with a finance concern that paid well, work that I liked, and my savings account grew at a satisfactory rate. Young and healthy and with no dependants I could look forward to a career of security and comfort. In my spare time I worked diligently at a mail order course leading to a degree in economics and better position. All very well.

Then one day my pal, by now quite intimate, told me about an "order" he belonged to, which he thought might interest me. A secret society, its members knew and experienced much that was denied to the common run – a world of new dimensions. He then offered to sponsor me for membership, the initiation a slight formality, the fee but nominal. The initiation was a not unpleasant pinprick, but which would leave a tell-tale mark recognizable to other members of the brotherhood.

I fell for it, and in days and weeks to come he was to administer many such pinpricks, each a pleasurable experience that I looked forward to and craved for more often. Each one cost a trifling sum; but so what! What good was money if it didn't bring you enjoyment?

The thing that bothered me, if only for a moment, was that I felt less keen about my work, and my concentration suffered. For days I did not touch my homework, feeling the delicious ease of "so what?" Another little shot in the arm and things would right themselves.

Then one day My Pal walked in. The door unlocked, he didn't bother to knock. "I've come to stay." With not so much as a "by your leave" he appropriated my favorite chair – in effect, took charge of my home. He rifled the fridge, slept in my bed, while I made-do on a couch in the living room. I sat and stood and acted as he ordered me, without much question. I was his utter slave.

In the days and weeks that followed (having lost my job) I did as he bid me, and he was insatiable. I used up my savings, and when that was done he started pawning my furniture, including all my better clothing. Came the time that I could not pay the rent and we were evicted. Even then he was no less demanding, and I was forced to measures I had not heretofore thought of – stealing from department stores and dealing with "fences" who would pay but a fraction of the worth of an article. He – My Pal – took everything I could gather, adding dire threats should I fail to make good. I stole once too often and in consequence spent three months in durance. That was hard to take, and I'm not recommending it. Emerging, with the word of the warden in my ear, "Don't come back," I was no sooner on the street than My Pal confronted me. "Good. Get to work!" But now I had a record, which made things more difficult. My Pal made no allowances for this. When I tried to remonstrate he blackened my eyes, adding what I already knew, that I had to find the means, or else.

I am writing this with the aid of a candle in the corner of an old freight shed, cold and hungry. What is ahead, God only knows.

Dedicated to all those who, out of curiosity or seeking a thrill, take that first "fix."

B. B., '64

CHAPTER 4

POET

Bogi loved poetry and read it extensively. His shelves contained a revolving collection of poems by everyone from the ancient Greeks to Robert W. Service. So it was natural that he should turn his own hand to writing verse. His poems found immediate success and were published in newspapers and magazines across the prairies.

Bogi wrote formal poetry, in addition to producing many clever rhymes and limericks. He was able to write for a diverse audience, whether a favoured nephew or readers of his newspapers. His verse dealt with a variety of subjects, ranging from family to nature and his violin. He also created verse from religious text. All of it revealed his sense of fun and his ability to capture pictures and ideas in words.

Not only did he write his own verse, but he enjoyed translating verse from Icelandic into English. His translations reveal his insight and sensitivity, as well as his mastery of the English language.

The following is a small sample of Bogi's poetry. The poem "Summer has Come" was first published in the *Treherne Times*. The second is a series called "Seasons," comprising four poems with Icelandic translations. Samples of his limericks and other verse have been included.

SUMMER HAS COME

A nickel's worth of wren pours out a million dollars' worth of melody between stints of lugging unwieldy sticks to her house in the maple outside the kitchen window. Many of these sticks are stolen from the nest of the mourning doves in a nearby tree, who don't appear to notice it. No matter; she fought for that house, and it's hers by right of conquest. The tree swallows wanted it, and the ubiquitous sparrows; but Jenny prevailed, so now she has it, for a song and a fight. A pair of robins in the next tree but one look on with detached and philosophical interest, and the orioles paid no heed. The ruby-throated hummingbirds – those unbelievably beautiful feathered jewels – flit in the currant bushes and the waxwings visit the spruces.

Summer has come to Manitoba.

The above first appeared in the editorial columns of the "Treherne Times," Manitoba, and was soon widely reprinted. Said John Bird, editor of the "Winnipeg Tribune": "This fine bit of writing is by Bogi Bjarnason, one of the province's most gifted newspapermen. ... It is refreshing to find that beauty may be translated into words that delight all who read."

THE SEASONS

SPRING

Spring, a comely maiden, curls her toes
Upon a touch of warmth within her frame --
A stirring of renewal of the force,
Regeneration coursing through her veins.
She rises from a couch of ease and rest
To genuflect, and stretch her arms aloft,
To yawn and gasp and greet advancing day,
Rejoicing in health and strength and grace,
To meet her lover Sol in glen and heath,
Clandestine or overt in shameless turn
Of active copulation and the means
Of launching and maturing yet again
Another generation, root to leaf,
Of pulsing Life, in everlasting round.

SUMMER

Summer, a woman grown and matronly,
Fecund and heavy with the seed and fruit
Of life in all its multifarious forms,
Now ripening to parturition and the stint
Of labor that is also ecstasy.
She cups her breasts and lifts her face to Sol,
A shining countenance in fervent prayer
For blessing of their numerous progeny.

She lifts her heavy horn of plenitude
That all may feed upon her ample store
And garner what is not consumed at once
Against the season when the elements
Conspire to spill and waste and abnegate
The handiwork of light and work and love.

AUTUMN

Mother Nature in her garb of leaves
Upon a day in autumn turns her glance
To scan her wardrobe and assess her means --
Probes through her closets and decides that change
Of raiment is an order of the day.
She doffs her dress of green and then selects
Habilement of gaudy hue to match
Her mood of wayward fancy and delight,
Lets fall the shady garment she has worn
Throughout a season when the spendthrift sun
His gentle rays has lavished on her back.
Now, womanly, she has the grace to blush
Before disrobing, when her paramour,
Stern Winter, comes and takes her to his bed.

HAUST

Modir jord, i skrudi laufa skryyd,
a skapadaegri sumars beinir sjon
ad skapsins fatasafni, og eygir allt;
pvi enn i nyjan buning klaedast skal,
og velja pann, sem a vid stund og stad.
A stol hun leggur graena kjolinn sinn
og velur annan odrum buinn lit,
sem a vid hennar smekk og, lundarfar
Hun afklaedist peim buning sem hun bar

a blidu sumri, pegar gjoful sol
ylgeislum stradi yfir hlid og hol.
Med roda a vanga, afklaedd, astarhyr, unnustann nyja litur
feimin, hljod: veturinn stranga, er henni hvilu byr.

WINTER

Winter, a grim and surly patriarch,
Stern -- visaged in his flowing beard of white,
Now brings to halt the labors of the year,
Arresting all alike that each may sleep
In hibernation or at slackened pace --
To gather strength and store up energy
For yet another lap of distance run.
He takes to spouse the daughter of the sun,
Big-bosomed Lady Summer whose "I do"
Ensures them progeny to nurse and rear --
The principle of Life in endless round.
Sternly regnant in his frigid way
He rules and disciplines with even hand
Till all are justly, properly amerced.

VETUR

Veturinn strangi, fadir helju og hums
hvasseygur strykur vangaskeggid grath
leggur i fjotur orku og athofn manus,
og allt, sem hraerist kvedur svefus i ro:
i dvalarham og draumaljufri kyrrd:
ad dad of Krafti safni gjorvalt lif,
til framtaks nyrra starfa um stundarbil.
Og astmor haus er sumargydjar sjalf.
Solardottir fegurst honum gaf
Frumstofn ars og proska er aldrei kraut:
Af pvi er lifsins saga jafnau ny.

*　　*　　*

THE TRAGEDY OF JENNY AND HER BROOD

Jenny is a wren – the most diminutive of birds according to Bill Shakespeare – who persisted in building her nest in the end of a drainpipe projecting from the basement wall within a foot or two from the kitchen door, where human traffic is constant. To select this venue for her sittings she scorned the two lovely wren houses built (to scale from the birdbook) and placed in the lawn maples for her consideration, with lettering over the entrance, "To Let for a Song."

Doubtless she and mate John had looked them over and discussed their advantages and appointments before deciding on the drainpipe, since they had been observed fluttering about the yard for days before the first twig appeared in the pipe-end. We shall never know what decided her, or them, to choose this idiotic location, from every viewpoint so badly suited to her purpose – at kneeheight from the walk and hardby a screendoor that slams noisily, directly exposed to the July sun and in plain sight, twig-ends projecting clumsily from the pipe, blatantly advertising what was afoot within. But then we haven't the wren's-eye view of the whole situation, and reason from a premise probably not recognized in her logic.

Was she deliberately seeking human companionship, protection, or even sponsorship? If so, her trust was not wholehearted, since she left the nest every time the door opened, which was often, to go back only when no one was about. But perseverance is the essence of accomplishment, and in time there were noises within the pipe.

When we peeked in several ungainly mouths – extraordinarily large and ungainly, considering – showed above the edge of the nest. By now Jenny was only going as far as the little crabapple tree across the walk when someone approached. Probably she had begun to think that this strange two-legged creature really deserved her trust.

We should have liked to write a happy ending to this, at least so far as launching the brood from the end of the drainpipe, with Jenny, and maybe papa John, chirping directions from the maples.

Alas, this was not to be. In an evil moment along came Jack and Joe (these are not their names), six and eight or so, spying the twigs projecting from the pipe-end. Presently the nest was on the ground, a sorry looking mess, the nestlings dead.

Flown are Jenny and John; gone is their faith in man.

* * *

HISTORY REPEATS ITSELF

He emerged from the rubble and saw
With eyes of a beast at bay --
Everything ravaged and raw
Save himself and his wife, and they

Had been spared from the hydrogen blast
By chance, being far underground,
While neighbors and kin and the rest
One and all were eternity-bound.

His world was devoid of life,
Consumed when the sky fell in.
Thus ended the world-wide strife,
Thus ended folly and sin.

He stared unbelieving at what
Now presented itself to his view,
And silently asked, What their lot,
What would they, what could they, do?

But Nature now put in her bill
With demands both familiar and stern:
If results are both frightening and ill,
They're something from which you must learn.

Your need at the moment is food
To sustain you for tasks ahead.
If your Eden is less than good,
You are still not entirely dead.

This Adam then called to his Eve:
"Is there anything ready to eat?"
She then went off to retrieve
The fruit so sustaining and sweet.

Returning with apple in hand
She held it out to her man,
Who, horrified, made the demand:
Let's not start THAT again!"

*   *   *

MY STRAD

(Apologies to Keats, Byron and others)

My Strad -- a thing of beauty and a joy;
If not forever, for a longer span
Than other things devised by mortal man.
Surpassing sweet of voice; from a boy
I've wantoned with its graces; they to me
Were a delight, and as a freshening sea
Have borne me up on waves of dulcet song,
Have spoken of ethereal things in tongue
Celestial, as of a heav'nly choir.
Fashioned of gut and glue, of wood and wire
Yet is endowed with soul -- a bit of Life
Destined to taste of rapture and of strife.
O noble instrument, offspring of mind and clod,
An idea wrenched from out the heart of God.

(Translation to Icelandic)

Strad minn, pu fegurd hlaust og hjartans yl,
pott hverfir sjon, pinn hljomur fylgir mer
lengur en listasmidi her.
Ljufasta roddin, pinna strengja spil.
Fra bernskutid eg tilbad strengleik pinn,
hans torfrar snertu mig, sem blaer um kinn.
A olduvaengjum, lett i ljufum song
pu last mer hjartans malum daegur long
pin helgiljof, sem leiftur stjornuskyr.
Po lim pu sert, med gornum, vid'og vir,
er vidkvaem salin pin og alfrjals er
Haborna gygja, af efni og anda manns,
ombrot fra sjalfu hjarta meistarans.

The label inside Bogi's violin, which I still have, reads: "Copia de
Antonius Stradivarius, 1725" (Sears, Roebuck, 1909. $25.)

*   *   *

THE SKIRT

Woman -- bless her heart! -- an after-thought
Rib-keeled and fashioned by an expert hand,
Superbly engineered to meet the stress
Of Life's demands in harsh environments
And tasks allotted only to her sex --
Perpetuation of the race, while man,
Male element, serves but to impregnate
And pace the corridor the while his wife
In parturition labors to bring forth
New life in constant, everlasting round.

In Adam, poor bastard, product of the dust,
Made by a 'prentice hand in cruder mould
(Before the Lord had really learned the trade),
Inadequate and lonely begs the Lord
To yield him company and partnership
To share the garden and its loveliness.

The Lord in generous, creative mood
Responded by creating Eve to meet
Adam's request to ease his loneliness --
Lovely, curvaceous Eve, a quickened bit
Of his own frame, and thereby doubly dear,
However vulnerable to the wiles
Of Satan's sleek and serpentine deceit
Bringing sin into the world of men.

Adam and his mate were yet to taste
(In pristine innocence and ignorance)
The fruit of guilty knowledge from the tree
That set their teeth on edge and opened eyes
To their own shame of having genitals
Offensive to the sight of God and man.

The fig came to their rescue with its leaves
To hide their nakedness and utter shame
As each the other viewed with shocked dismay.

Barred from Eden, hand-in-hand they roamed
The wilderness of "outer space" and lost,
Babes in the woods and in confusion flung
Upon resources all within themselves,
Bewildered as the children of the tale
Adrift and at the mercy of the sea.

Now raiment was their prime and dire need
To cover tender derma and preserve
Their new-acquired modesty from harm.
So when her mate adopted pantaloons
Eve spun the fabric for a flaring skirt
For maximum accessibility
To charms concealed yet advertised as such
By subtle, artful means and innate guile,
Swishing and whirling in the Dervish dance
Till hem is raised and buttocks stand revealed.

The drab and dull attire of the male,
The gaudy plumage of the distaff side
Sets forth the age-old question, Who woos who?
And Echo answers, Woman lures the man.

So Eve and all her daughters wear the skirt,
More easily to squat and offset
The penis-envy of the gentle sex.
Thus the skirt, so functional and free,
Symbol of desired fertility.

*   *   *

MISCELLANEOUS QUATRAINS

My current financial affairs are in
A mess.
But one thing my dollar still buys
Is less.

*

Solvency isn't just a feat,
It's demands are, Live and learn.
Expenses are not hard to meet --
I meet them everywhere I turn.

*

Unlike the dog a man contends
'Gainst fellow or the throng.
The reason that a dog has friends --
Its tail wags, not its tongue.

*

DOMESTIC SPAT

I'm reduced to curds
In this noisy bout.
She's "Too mad for words"
So she pours them out.

*

I cleaned my party dress with that
A pretty deft manoeuver.
Now, say, what will remove the spots
Left by the spots-remover.

*

EASY PAYMENTS

Why not enjoy all the best
In country or in town,
When all it takes to line your nest
Is just a little down?

*

Outlooks change throughout a lengthy span,
But ever the man is fighting for his name.
A boy smokes to prove that he is a man.
He quits in upper age -- objective still the same.

*

AN OLD-AGE PENSIONER SPEAKS

A financial debacle is pending
(The structure's exhibiting cracks):
I want a check on all government spending --
I also want government checks.

*

To apply the proper "finish" to your car
Use Method, to be sure to do it right.
Most satisfactory are these two, by far:
Use lacquer if by day, and liquor if by night.

*

A manchild in infancy coos or he howls,
In ladhood he plays with his pup.
But when a boy starts playing with "dolls"
It's a sign that he's growing up.

*

On my usual way to the bank
With my usual bagful of talents,
I met up with Freddy and Frank,
And forthwith I lost my balance.

*

WORDS THAT DON'T SEEM
TO BELONG TOGETHER

Shown a piece of brick-a-brack,
I'm apt to comment, rather smugly:
"Nice and all," and then, alack! --
"A little big," and "pretty ugly."

*

His gods are Money and the Mine,
The Market Page and the Dotted Line.
He daily prays in his private shrine
And crosses himself with the dollar $ign.

*

Remember the stuff that they fed us
(Lieutenant to private jerk),
To save us from the feminine favors --
I swear, it's beginning to work.

[One 1918 soldier to another, recalling that
soldiers were said to have been fed a drug
that suppressed sexual desire.]

*

The rain it raineth during thaws
Upon the just and unjust fella.
But more upon the just, because
The unjust has the just's umbrella.

[Adapted from saying attributed to
Benjamin Franklin.]

*

A toper's lot is hard to bear,
What with 'nerves' and head that's sore
Swearing off he tears his hair,
Moaning after the night before.

*

YOU DON'T GET AWAY WITH ANYTHING

Stretch the truth, tell outright lies,
Maintain you're pure as mountain tarn.
Pull the wool over your good wife's eyes --
She'll still see through the yarn.

*

Pit pedestrian 'gainst the auto;
He may survive from day-to-day
"Live dangerously," says a motto.
Is there any other way?

*

SHE TRUMPED HIS ACE

A witness to this sordid brawl.
In anger and in sorrow --
I'd like to be a fly on the wall
When comes the dawn tomorrow.

*

AFTER VIEWING AN "ABSTRACT" PAINTING

No doubt my temper is at fault,
Or I'm not in the mood for it.
So hide the damn thing in a vault;
Hanging is too good for it.

*

HYMN TUNE, "THE TIE THAT BINDS"

The maker of a legal document
When meeting its demands too late he finds
(Whether a purchase or a "place to rent")
It's the pesky little 6-point type that binds.

*

Whatever else you learn at school,
Retain, observe the Golden Rule.
Tread warily, eyes open, then
Write no woman, wrong no man.

*

Now women are taking UP Law
In numbers adopting the Gown.
They have never stood greatly in awe
Of its precepts, while laying it DOWN.

*

Maybe the horse
Was a bit analytic.
Bad manners, of course,
But gad, what a critic!

[A horse, part of a stage pageant, so forgot itself
that it committed an indiscretion. Apologies to
Sir Thomas Beecham.]

*

EVEN IN PARADISE

When Adam took off for some roaming
In Eden's voluminous park,
Then turned his steps to come homing:
"I've just been away for a lark."
But Eve thought it more than a teaser,
Alerted to masculine fibs.
When Adam attempted to please her,
She insisted on counting his ribs.

*

LIKE WASHINGTON AND LINCOLN

Some things I do not understan',
Of mice and men, their ways --
Funny how many famous men
Are born on holidays.

*

On this era of rising prices
On costs that are already high,
I hoard my shekals and ducats
And let the rest of the world go buy.

*

I dreamt I went to heaven
And was greeted with a shout
(In strident tones 'twas given):
"For heaven's sake keep out!"

*

LAMENT OF A
SMALL-TOWN EDITOR

Once there was an editor
Who hadn't a single creditor --
Um-huh!

Subscribers all were "in advance";
He never gave, or took, offence --
Um-huh!

Ads galore his columns filled;
Accounts were as promptly paid as billed --
Um-huh!

And there was amity all about,
For he pleased the parson and pleased the lout --
Um-huh!

He dwelt at peace with his fellowmen,
As only the perfect will, or can --
Um-huh!

And all this (so the stories go)
Was far away and long ago --
Um-huh!

He dwelt in the fabled land of Oz,
That never will be and never was --
Um-huh!

*

HYPOCRITES ALL

(On completion of reading
"Lady Chatterlcy's Lover.")

We deplore and we deplore --
Make of impotence a virtue --
All pornographic lore
And writings that may hurt you,

Especially latterly
The story of Lady Chatterley.

We deplore and we condemn
Such "filth" in printed form.
We demand the censors stem
This menace to our norm.

We deplore, and then we peek
And furtively we scan,
Not knowing what we seek
But braced for shocks. And then

Delighted with it all
We deplore even more.
To heaven goes our call
As we deplore, deplore --

Especially latterly
The morals of Lady Chatterley.

*

MAN IN A HURRY

(Apologies to Kainn)

I know a man, a sturdy man,
Whose speed is so superior
Around the tree so fast he ran
He glimpsed his own posterior.

*

CHAPTER 5

FAMILY MAN

Bogi Bjarnason was an intensely private man who shared little of himself. He limited his circle of friends to a few individuals whose friendship he maintained for years. He certainly avoided, whenever possible, public events or gatherings other than those for family.

Bogi's reserve extended even to his immediate family. He never openly showed physical affection to his children or wife. The love he felt was carefully concealed behind an aloof demeanour.

Yet there were times when he did communicate his emotions. On these occasions, he used writing to convey his feelings, the paper affording him the distance he desired. This writing took the form of poems, limericks, and speeches that he addressed to family members.

From verbal jousting with his nephew to poems dedicated to his new-born grandchildren, these pieces are all the more special for being so rare. Following are samples including poems and limericks.

*This was written to Clarence J. Houston, Father's brother-in-law,
who, being allergic to maple pollen in spring, would visit Vancouver
every year during the budding period.*

I sing to you of maples
And swiftly-flowing sap
And allergies and pollen,
And places on the map;

The effluvium of maple
That "sends" you with a yen
For the calm and broad Pacific
And peaks in Darien.

I sing of the weeping optic,
The sneeze stentorian,
Of misery, and the marvel
Of relief Victorian.

I sing to you of prairies
Dotted with maple groves,
Of gossamer in the autumn
And ragweed in shady coves.

I sing of fecund nature,
Of perils in vast array,
And maples -- oh! the maples --
In the merry month of May.

So come where of old stout Cortez
Gazed with a wild surmise,
And Captain George Vancouver
Tarried, with high emprise;

Where Stanley and Hastings and Granville
Found haven in days of yore,
And Burrard and Juan de Fuca
Explored the virgin shore;

Where nature is kind, yet fruitful,
Where quiet and health abound,
Where the wind is stilled, and the seasons
Are all in their turn renowned;

Where the Lions and Hollyburn tower,
Where grandeur yields only to charm,
Where conifers march up the hillsides
And the sun and the air are warm.

So come in the spring, *mon ami*,
Et ux, away from it all;
Leave Care in the dust of your sabots
And take to the timbers tall.

Clarence's reply to Bogi's poem:

The beauties of Vancouver,
If you can see through the rain
Will no doubt once more entice us
When the spring comes round again.

When the sap is in the maple
And the pollen on the trees
I'll be thinking of you often
When the first sneeze makes me wheeze.

Should the moisture lachrynasal
And the rattles in my chest

Really get the better of me
Then I'll point the old car west.

And Sigga echoes "Ditto"
If that's what "et ux" means.
But wld sooner come to see you
Than to peer at foggy scenes.

or   And Sigga sitting by my side
If that's what "et ux" means
We'll journey out to see you
Not peer at foggy scenes.

To Clarence, acknowledging the gift of a Christmas tie:

ON A CRAVAT

A thoroughly frabjous creation
Now graces my front elevation
In the shape of a tie -- a stark horror,
A nightmare, a weapon of war, or
A symbol of all that is frightful;
Unless (a grim thought) it's the rightful
And fit punishment for my errors
A foretaste of Judgement Day terrors.

The obverse of the coin is brighter,
The top of the cloud is much lighter;
The beholder's eye is distracted,
To the tie his attention's attracted;
He sees not the face that's above it --
Therefore I love it.

To the same, in acknowledgement of another Christmas tie:

THE WAGES OF SIN IS --
A CHRISTMAS TIE

My sins are both varied and many
And all of a cardinal hue.
But blatant or sordid or canny,
I've given the devil his due.

There's no escaping the payment;
You writhe and you flee and you fend;
You change your locale and your raiment:
Your sins will find you out in the end.

Imagine the ultimate horror
('Neath a face like a potter's mistake);
An outright inducement to war, or
Fit only for "Finnegan's Wake."

The donor (my sins' retribution),
A culprit, a lout and a knave;
In seeking my sins' absolution
I still hope to pee on his grave!

COMMERCIAL PRINTING
MACHINE COMPOSITION

BOGI BJARNASON, PUBLISHER
TELEPHONE 116

TREHERNE — MANITOBA

Dec. 21, 1933

Dear Clarence:-

   You buy my ties and I buy yours. In that sweet spirit of unreasonableness characteristic of Christmas madness I am sending two ties in rretaliation (with one r) of past years' outrages. As Ben Burnie says, "I hope you like them", knowing full well that you won't. Anyway you started this thing and it's your turn to suffer.

   They cost $2.50 for both, so their trade-in value should be about half of that. Hold out for at least that much.

   I haven't had my Christmas malaise yet, but it's about due. Dora says I get sick for spite, but honestly I am not as cantankerous as all that. Come to think of it, psychopathic people experience their deepest gloom about this time of year, so maybe this is all quite the natural thing with me.

   Anyway we are all well at present and I haven't been drunk for a week. Tell Sigga that Amma died recently and was buried at Blaine, Wash. Died in her sleep after a day's mild illness.

   With cheery greetings

    Bogi

To C.J.Houston, M.D., of Yorkton, Saskatchewan, on the occasion of his election to Fellowship, American College of Surgery – FACS.

CASE HISTORY

A man, abroad ere dawning cracks,
Picks up a brace of carpet tacks
In his bare tootsies, then "Alacks!"
And sounds off much like Erna Sacks.
His wail the ambient welkin racks.
He hies to seek a certain quack's
Advice, who promptly cuts and hacks
With lance and scalpel, saw and axe,
Nor his determined onslaught slacks
Until his patient's spirit cracks.
A skilled and learned artifex
In all ills human, either sex,
He binds the wounds, then mutters, "*Pax
Vobiscum* -- fee is ten plus tax."
And that is how he won his FACS.

And Clarence's reply:

Friend Bogi doth wax most facetious,
And slings quite a barb in his line.
But no one has ever made me
No matter how bad his rhyme.

So I thought I'll just write the bounder;
Name weapons, the time, and the place.
And just put him right in the matter,
And give him the FACS of the case.

F stands for fellow, an old English phrase,
   describing a FELLOE in OLDE ENGLESE ways.
A for America –- God forgive me,
   I was never a nigger, nor yet a Yankee.
C is for College –- you know well of that,
   after paying the shot for each Bjarnason brat.
S is for Surgeon –- they nick you at times,
   your pocket book, 'pendix, or whatever rhymes.

Now if you read this, you'll sure need your specs,
For even my druggist can't read my Rx.

Bogi to Clarence, acknowledging the gift of a crock of Queen Anne Scotch Whiskey:

I wag an inferior maxillary
In praise of buxom good Queen Anne.
To me Victoria, Bess and Mary
Are only dames who "also ran."

Of all good women, wives and misses,
There's one comes first, *sans* if or but;
I thrill to her ardent, heady kisses
From pedal digits to occiput.

To same, acknowledging receipt of a book by John Tyre, Christmas, 1950:

In a world that's all twisted and screwy --
With Stalin and Trueman and Dewey --
I sit by the fire with my fiddle and TYRE
And a glassful or two of Drambuie.

Clarence to Bogi:

Birthday Greetings -- ne Plus Ditto
It matters not how old you are,
Or whether you were 'aged in bond',
The spirit that you bring with you
Is always fresh as Mountain Dew.
So birthday brings you greetings fond,
Expressed by friends with Johnny Dewer.

But as the nite is getting colder,
And whiskey's watered here in Sask.,
We've clothed the stuff in jacket warm,
And capped his head and gloved his arm.
No more protection c'd you ask,
Drink it before you're any older.

C.J.H.

To Bernice L. with the gift of a desk clock, Christmas, 1949:

THE MESSAGE OF THE CLOCK

I greet you, Comrade, face to face,
As down the corridor of days
That make up our brief span of years,
Bringing gladness, trial, tears;
Counting the moments as they pass,
Under Father Time's duress --
You in wrinkles and aging cells,
I in gears and wear that tells
On even the stoutest -- brass and steel
As well as flesh. But woe or weal,

Let's meet them bravely, you and I,
Facing front, nor question why.
In sunshine and in stormy weather,
Bernice, let's mark time together.

Written for Joan's and my first son:

CHRISTOPHER JOHN

Brightly shines on Hist'ry's page
The name of JOHN; in every age,
In varied forms and spellings quaint
It marks or graces rogue and saint:
Ivan, Ewan, Jean and Jon,
In combination or alone.

(And as for CHRISTOPHER: There's Wren,
And Fry and Marlowe, Morley -- men
Who built, and wrote, and fought, and scaled,
Delved and painted, sang and sailed.)

There's John of Magna Carta fame,
John the Baptist, John -- the name
Rings down the corridors of time
In declamations and in rhyme.

Kings and popes have borne it well,
On stately throne, in cloister cell.
An honoured name, its spurs has won --
Let's leave it to CHRISTOPHER JOHN.

Grandpop B.

Written for our second son:

PETER SMITH

PETER -- a name to conjure with
In history as well as myth.
A rock on which the Church is built;
It launched the Crusades; owns the guilt
Of countless wars; its bearers span
The ages. Its illustrious kith --
Peter the Great and Peter Pan.

SMITH -- his name is legion, so
He's of the common run whom God
Loves in a special way. All know
The worldwide paths his feet have trod.

So Peter Smith will make his way
Towards the heights his namesakes scaled,
The sunnier uplands where all may
The guerdon win, and be to greatness hailed.

Grandpop B.

Written for our daughter:

ELIZABETH ANNE

Alike the legendary bird
Is our ELIZABETH THE THIRD,
Plumed and decked and ornamented
With queenly graces, godly granted.
Thus attired she has the merit
To most appropriately wear it.

Namesake of another queen
(Hight ANNE, of distant Aberdeen);
Thus royal blood flows in her veins,
By right of which she truly reigns.

Grandpop B.

See-saw limericks Bogi Bjarnason and Emil Bjarnason, one of Bogi's nephews:

B.B. --
That the Russian Bear is in Chosen
Is now past the stage of supposin'.
I pee on his might
From a very great height,
And I hope that in falling it's frozen.

E.B. --
It isn't the Bruin, you fool,
Whose droppings are falling on Seoul,
But an Eagle in fright
At the very great height
Of a dragon he took for a Mule.

B.B. --
The free world gets littler and littler
As bit and by bit and by bitler
The Chinee and Bear
A pestiferous pair
Keep gobbling it up a la Hitler.

E.B. --
When you speak of the Free World, please note
The "freedom" is strictly a quote,
For Yankees can eat
Only if they repeat
The Truman Doctrine by rote.

B.B. --
Saith the "fool" in his heart, There's no peace
While Genghis Khan uses the squeeze
To grab and to take
"For security's sake"
The neighbors, for Finland to Greece.

E.B. --
The Kahn Brothers, Genghis and Otto,
Have grabbed up more land than they ought to.
"From offices swank
In a Manhattan bank
We run Finland and Greece", is their motto.

B.B. --
Said Andrei Vishinsky to Joe:
"We should be on the Rhine and the Po.
Shout PEACE far and wide,
Then take them in stride.
It's a beautiful system, ho, ho!"

Father enjoyed arguing about Communism with his brother Paul and sister-in-law Dora and extended the habit to their children.

UNTITLED

Dates and anniversaries
Have ever plagued my life:
I'm the absent-minded husband
Of a presents-minded wife.

This undoubtedly did plague him all his life, as he very seldom gave anyone a present at any time, Christmas, birthday, or anniversary. On the occasion of his 25th wedding anniversary, he did send Bernice money to buy a present for Dora, leaving the choice to her. Bernice purchased a silver dresser set; brush, mirror, nailfile, buffer, etc., now in the possession of Elizabeth Stone (Bjarnason). Another exception was a gift of cash at the time of my wedding.

CHAPTER 6

CORRESPONDENT

Throughout his newspaper career, Bogi had the opportunity to engage with people through editorials and other published works. In these, he wrote about the most important issues of the day, including politics, religion, and war. This type of communication was vital to a man who had so much to say about humankind and the machinations of modern society.

Following his retirement from the newspaper business, Bogi continued to write for pleasure and to keep up his skills. However, while he wrote some verse and short compositions, he turned increasingly to letter writing. Correspondence became his primary means of engaging with the world outside his immediate family and home, a means no longer available through professional avenues.

Through letters, this very private man communicated with some very famous people. His graceful compliments and often pithy commentary generated responses from no less than Harry S. Truman and Yehudi Mehuhin.

This section includes some samples of letters written to friends as well as to some of the great names in history, along with, in some cases, their response.

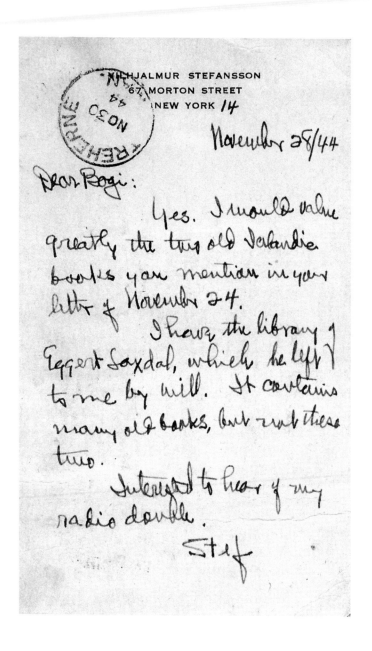

VILHJALMUR STEFANSSON
67 MORTON STREET
NEW YORK 14

November 28/44

Dear Bogi:

Yes. I would value greatly the two old Icelandic books you mention in your letter of November 24.

I have the library of Eggert Saxdal, which he left to me by will. It contains many old books, but not these two.

Interested to hear of my radio double.

Stef

4053 West 32nd Ave.
Vancouver,B.C., Feb. 15, '53

Mr. J. Davidson
Wynyard, Sask.

Dear Joe:--

Yesterday, the Good Wife being about to fill the place with
socialite ladies I fled, taking to the Queen's highway in my chariot
for a bit of roaming. Finding myself out in Surrey I turned up the
hill to look in at Valgerdur's for a spot of coffee and a look-back
at olden times. She told me that you were now quite in the dark, and
also that were taking it with a calm and acceptance of the inevitable
that would be beyond most of us. That is surely a comfort, plus the
fact I know Rikka is a rock of strength in your affliction. So with
my condolences go my congratulations for those great blessings, your
wife and your own psychological attitude.

Driving homeward I tried to recall Milton's sonnet# on his
blindness, with which you are no doubt familiar, which begins:
"When I consider how my light is spent
Ere half my days, in this dark world and wide
And that one talent which is death to hide
Lodged with me useless ..."
-- recalled, too, that he went right on, dictating to his daughter
both the "Paradise Lost" and "Paradise Regained" and most of his other
work in total darkness.But the story goes that he was not patient
about it. So maybe you've got something Milton hadn't.

Since coming# to the age when the mind tends to look back-
wardI sometimes find myself recalling times and things long gone,
when you and I and the world were yet young, and Europe and all its
works were as distant as Sirius. "Them was the days," we fondly
think, forgetting that oldsters about us even then were harking back
to the days of their youth. "So runs the world away" at bewildering
speed, and the best we can do about it is to grow philosphical as
apparently you have had the grace to do. Wish I could say that of
myself.

But to change to a lighter vein.There you are on the illim-
itable prairies and here I am beyond the Rockies, an upthrust of the
floating crust when our earth was beginning to cool. The scientists
tell us that our floating island collided with another, which later
solidified into the Asian mass, and, the crust buckling upward the
Rockies and Andes resulted. Be that as it may, a profile map of western Canada is intriguing. British Columbia is small in area compared
with the prairies, but I maintain that this is illusionary. Your prairies are just spread out thin, while we have depth. The mean average
thickness of of B.C. from sunshine to sea level is 5600 ft. The higher
you go into the mountains the meaner it gets. Washed down and rolled
out to the same thinness as your prairies, B.C. would reach all the
way from Cape Horn to the NATO Conference with enough left over to
flap in prairie wind. On the other hand, at the thickest point in

Saskatchewan an average screwbilled angleworm could bore through to the bottom in one wiggle.

So of our excess warmth we export chinook winds to Alberta and get in return Social Credit. Now what kind of trade is that!. .... (Dots denote a 24-hour hiatus, other matters intervening.)

This Soc. Credit is something of a phenomenon, which nobody, not even its most vocal votaries, pretends to understand, mixed up as it is with religion at its zaniest, yet has strength likes nobody's business. It walloped our Gooley premier, Bjorn Ingimar Jonsson, in the derriere at the last election in B.C. with a force that left a considerable part of the electorate gasping. The theory is that so many wanted to register protests against the government, and so voted for something else without meaning to vote that something else in, then waking up the morning after to learn that too many had had the same idea. So now we are stuck with it. -- Funny, the twists things take sometimes.

At times I get to thinking what abject creatures of circumstances we are. Harking back, while out driving the other day, I recalled that on a summer's day in Anno Domini 1913 a certain Joe Davidson, from Sinclair, came up to my room on Maryland St. in Wpg. to suggest that I return with him for a spot of threshing. I would surely have gone with him except that a day or so previously a man had broached to me the idea of going for him down to Mountain, N.D., to look after a business he had just acquired there. Now if the timing of these two incidents had been a trifle different (and I had nothing to do with either) I should not have gone to Mountain and thence to Wynyard, etc. The tenor of my life and activities thenceforward would most likely have been radically different. So when the poet says, "I am the master of my fate, I am the captain of my soul", I feel inclined to say, "Yeah; but don't leave out the force of happenstance". And it isn't Fate, either; just pure, unadulterated chance.

Strange, isn't it, the tricks our so-called minds play upon us at times? Thus since I came to the age of the backward look, I find that certain no-account, irrelevant incidents stand out, clearly etched, while others, much more important and significant, are comparatively vaguely outlined. At the moment I recall, as if it had been yesterday, leisurely driving in a lumber wagon over a stony, rutted trail along the western edge of Sec. 24 heading down toward a shack on Sec. 12, inconsequentially talking with my companion, one Johann D., when he started humming, rather tunelessly, "Meet Me In St. Louis, Louie". The recollection has neither beginning nor end, and is, for all I can see, quite meaningless. Yet there it is.

But another recollection impinges. The scene is a large room in a farm home in western Pembina County. In the corner is a bed with the figure of a young man with a terrific shock of unruly, reddish hair. He is gasping, barely holding his own, each intake of breath more sharp than its suspiration. In the room beside the home folks are a number of the Bjarnason boys and Doc. Joe, a dozen at least, sharing with the pneumonic patient the scant supply of oxygen seeping in through cracks along windows and doors from the

wintry blast outside. The group is silent, except for the labored
breathing of the patient, and obviously waiting -- for something.
Presently a team and cutter stop at the door and a man in a heavy
furcoat opens the door. He stops there as the blast of hot, vitiated
air hits him. For a moment he pauses, the door wide, and not a word
is uttered. Then Doc. Joe speaks up, with impressive dignity and
a shaking head: "Hann drepr 'ann!" Again, my recollection of the incident ends there, quite without rhyme or reason. The man in the
fur coat was a Dr. McQueen, of Milton, if memory serves me right.

A lot of water has gone over the dam since that far day,
and you and I have floated with it, at times half-submerged and
at others, spinning in side eddies with little forward progress.
Well, they tell us -- those who pretend to know -- that even the
longest river eventually reaches the sea. I for one have long since
ceased speculating about it.

So here I'm on the third page, single-spaced at that, of
what set out to be brief "Hello!" in passing from one oldster to
another.Forgive my verbosity, realizing only that I mean well.
And to Rikka a kiss on the cheek from an ancient friend who has
only the fondest recollections of the various times our trails
crossed. It may well be that we shall not meet again this side the
Styx, and in that case my final word shall be Adieu and best wishes
from an old friend --

                                         BOGI BJARNASON

Bogi in his 80th year.

4053 West 32nd Ave.
Vancouver,B.C.,
Dec. 31, '53 A.D.

Mr. Johann G. Davidson
Wynyard, Sask.

Friend Joe.--

Somewhen early in this year of Grace (or is it disgrace?)
now fast drawing to a close ("Ring out, wild bells, and let him die")
I wrote to you in a <u>final word</u> spirit, if memory serves me, as if we
might not have occasion to meet again this side the Styx. But here we
are still, both more or less alive if somewhat handicapped for full
enjoyment of the privilege. Glory be! If I then wrote in a <u>morte te
salutamus</u> mood I take it all back, fully resolved that by the end of
the Glad New Year, now only some 14 hours in the future, we shall
both be "ofar fjörs a leið". -- As a distant friend always ends his
letters: "Hoping you are the same".

As I remember it, the occasion of the letter referred to
was that I had fled the house when the Good Wife was about to fill
the house of an afternoon with socialite ladies and taken to roaming
the queen's highways, looking in on Valgerdur out in Surrey for a
dish of coffee and learning that you were quite in the dark. Well,
history does repeat itself, for it is but a week or two back that I
was again out in Surrey for precisely the same reason, turned up the
same hill and again partook of the cup that cheers, spiked with another look-back at olden times. I learned that she had but recently
looked in on you and found both Rikka and you in good case, all things
considered, and in no way downhearted. So encore on the Glory be!
Let's count our blessings.

Writing this in a bit of hang-over after the collective
madness we sometimes call "The Spirit of Christmas", I find my inward
eye a bit jaundiced and given to deploring, with a "What's the world
coming to!" There are wars and rumors of wars, and there's no health
in it. But after pinching my arm I ask: "What have you to kick about?"
I do, though, grumbling about the poor engineering of the body the
good Lord or somebody gave us to live during our span of years. I invariably toy with this thought during the daily shave, feeling with
Omar:

"Ah, Love, could you and I with Him conspire
To grasp this sorry Scheme of Things entire,
    Would we not shatter it to bits and then
Remould it nearer to the Heart's Desire!"

We get no "repeat" on eyes or teeth or stomach -- things we really
need -- and our hair falls out on top. But whiskers!! God save the
mark. Here I've been slapping mine down most every day for half a
century -- and look at them! Vigorous as ever. There's persistence
for you. And they're the one thing about our whole physical appar-

atus we could best do without. So nature says, You shave, or else!
But the fact is certainly established that the Lord, or whoevever
designed us, meant that the male of homo sapiens should wear hair
on his jowls. Never mind his eyes, his teeth, his stomach, his arms.
Lost or damaged they don't grow in, much as man needs them in the
business of living. But hair on his face? Oh, man! -- But enough of
that. I could appropriately take notice of the persistence of nature in other ways, for near my elbow as I write on this last day of
the year is a bowl of gorgeous roses picked in our back yard only
yesterday. How's that for persistence!

    With a New Year, by the calendar, on the doorstep, I yet
persist, as maybe I shouldn't, to look over my shoulder at things
that were but are no more. The pundits tell me that's characteristic
of one who sits around waiting for The Man With the Scythe. If I protest that, it isn't done with too much conviction, for there's more
than a grain of truth in it. So what the heck -- I, who was young
once am young no longer, and can dance only in retrospect with the
belles at midnight frolics " á Tiu" or at John Abrahamssons, with
Abbi in a wheel chair playing "Turkey in the Straw" and Joe D. "calling off". "Allemande Left" and "Swing Your Partner". There was a long
and hard day of work behind and another like it ahead. But again,
what the heck! Youth would be served, and we could take it. My slave-
driving brother was a hard task-master, but considerate and himself
worked harder and longer than any. And somehow those years at Antler-
Sinclair have for me as great an appeal of nostalgia as other and
more exciting periods of my life. I can't explain that; but that's
the way of it. And always you and Rikka figure in those recollections,
invariably as good and considerate friends.

    So, to repeat, here we're at another year's end by the
calendar. So here and now I pre-empt your attention for another year-
end missive twelve months hence. In the meantime hold the fort against
all "slings and arrows of outrageous fortune" that may come your way,
as I plan to do. And with this determination go my best wishes to
both of you -- the wishes of an ancient and sincere friend.

                                            BOGI BJARNASON

4053 West 32nd Ave.
Vacouver 8, B.C., Canada
Oct. 17, '54

Dr. Vilhjalmur Stefansson
c/o Dartmouth College
Hanover, N.H.

Friend V.S. --

My thanks for your letter reclippings of Stanley Burke articles in THE VANCOUVER SUN. Shall be looking for your essays in
NATURAL HISTORY, which I see regularly. Have been trying to run
down Supt. Larsen (R.C.M.P.), skipper of the 120' vessel ST.ROCHE,
now being retired to a permanent (dry) dock in our Stanley Park
after circumnavigating the N.A. continent and making the North-
west Passage in both directions. Shall try to "pump" him for his
estimate of the Eskimos and then report to you. (A letter addressed to him c/o the R.C.M.P. here would no doubt reach him, so maybe
a request directly from you would get better results.) He should
have a wealth of northern lore to impart, especially about how the
natives are adjusting to civilization since you were there.

(Have just finished reading the new book about Lorne Knight.
And he died of scurvy !!!)

Now some personal gossip.--

Your sister Rosa was here on a lengthy visit recently, pert
and lively and apparently in good health. Inga's daughter Pauline
(Laufey) and brother joe are our neighbors here (341 West King Edward St.). She's a very fine and lovely person, apparently independently wealthy. Lulli, the eldest of three, died here a year or
two ago. -- Still no gap in the Bjarnason line. John (eldest, about
80), Triggvi (on the old homestead) and sister Gunnel are at Mountain, Julli at Wynyard, Sask., and Paul and I here. (My wife is a
daughter of Geir Christianson whom you may remember from Grand Forks
days.) Soren and Malla (Hjaltalin) in Old Folks' Home at Mountain,
Soren very feeble, as are the Bjagi boys, Oli and Dori, though both
still on the old homestead, as also Mundi Nupdal, across the creek
from the Stefansson homestead. But Time is getting in its licks on
all. -- Paul, by the way, is getting out another book of poetry,
300 pp., translations from Icelandic. -- Selah.

Think I am now on the track of the most elusive Larsen, and
if and when I do catch up with him will let you know if he says
anything worth repeating.

Sincerely

Bogi Bjarnason

4053 West 32nd Ave.
Vancouver 8, B.C.,Canada
Nov. 4, 1954

Dr. Vilhjalmur Stefansson
Dartmouth College
Hanover, N.H.,U.S.

Friend V.S.--

My thanks for your letter of Oct. 25th. Glad to learn
that you are in touch with Supt. Larsen. My chase of him had
been fruitless anyway. But there is another chap here, Dr.
Chas. E. Davies, 2525 Pine St. Vancouver, eye surgeon, who
has spent some time in the North, as far east as Baffin, in
the service of the government. He has a fund of information
on what contact with civilization is doing to the Eskimos in
remote parts, some of which might be of interest to you.
When I suggested to him that he relate directly to you the
gist of what he told me, he said he would be glad to do so,
but would prefer to get an outline of what would be of greatest value to you in his field. If you care to contact him
I am sure you will find him most cooperative.

About your sister Rosa. -- Have been out of touch with
her a great many years, but had a lengthy talk with her on
her visit here this past summer. She appeared to be in good
health, both mentally and physically, and less weighted with
cares now that she has got rid of the farm and lives in retirement in the Village of Mozart, Sask., but near her daughter and grandchildren, one of whom makes her home with her.
Her husband, Johann Josephson, died in the early forties.
Their issue: three sons, one daughter. Sons Vilhjalmur and
Johann live in Victoria, B.C., Marvin in Saskatoon, Sask.,
and daughter in Mozart, all married. Your sister Inga died
in Calgary in '44, and eldest son, Lulli, in retirement here,
about two years ago. Pauline (Laufey) and Johann live in Vancouver (341 King Edward West).

About the Lorne Knight book. Of course it was PECHUK, "new"
only to myself, which I had picked up at our branch library and
returned without noting date of publication.

Interesting to learn about the autobiography. Think you
might stress your discovery that the earth is round (if slightly
flattened at the polls), which Mercator and the mariners ignored.
-- And my thanks for the pamphlet "Arctic in Fact and Fable",
which I devoured with interest. More power to your elbow!

Sincerely

BOGI BJARNASON

Encl., various
clippings

4053 West 32nd Ave.
Vancouver 8, B.C.
Dec. 19, A.D. 1954

Mr. Johann Davidson
Wynyard, Sask.

Friend J.D.--

Salút og þökk fyrir gamalt og gott.

Ef minni mitt rekur rett til, hripaði eg þér bréf um jóla-
leytið i fyrra, og lofaðist pa til (en kannske með tunguna ut i gul-
num, pvi að nu eru hver jol lansfe) ad skrifa per enn einu sinni a
naestu jolum, vaerum vid pa baðir "ofar fjors a linu". Jæja, nu
dregur skriftatima og dypsta skammdegi, og kvoldinu pegar spilað
var "pook" hja David og Margreti.

But now my memory of the recent is not as keen as it was
in those halcyon days "a Barningi", so that what I wrote to you a
twelve-month back is hazy. Yet I recall making a date with you, ex-
horting you to hold the fort, as I hoped to do, against whatever jav-
elins the arch-enemy might choose to direct at us, "ancient of days"
that we are. Well I hope he has not concentrated a flight of his arrows against you, or if he did, that your armor turned them. That's
from the heart.

Wish I could say that he had made no determined foray against
me within the past year. I can't. I think he has made a most dastardly
jab, and found a chink in my coat of mail. Last spring, following a
bout with the flu, I developed a persistent ache in the shoulders,
which I recognized as the kind that plagued Bjorn Illugason and Hall-
dor "Sko" the winters I was chore-boy at their homes, straddling the
turn of the century, treated with suction cups made of ramshorns. My
nephew, an M.D., calls it bursitis; what I call it is not fit to print,
and shocks distaff side. -- Seems it's a hardening, or something, of
cartilage in the shoulder-joints, impinging on nerves passing down
the arms, which shout bloody murder. It's the kind of thing that sends
ageing plutocrats to spas to take "the waters". Not being a plutocrat
but having the temperament of a vertiginous hamadryad and the vocabu-
lary of a depraved sot I have taken no water cure, but confined the
treatment to lurid descriptions and taking the name of the Lord in vain.
That doesn't help much, unless there be a therapeutic equivalent to
expletives. But close friends are avoiding me in droves, and the wife
says I'm not fit to live with. Could be. Ho hum.

All about me there is evidence of a recurrence of the mass
insanity of Christmas; a binge of no small proportions is about to
engulf us. The goose hangs high, and there's no end of Goodwill, printed on illions of cards the mailman brings. And except that the Pope is
hiccuping again, "God's in His heaven, All's right with the world",
So what's a pair of aching shoulders! I ask you; but don't tell me.

I ask a lot of questions that have no answers. His Holiness burps and hiccups, and I damn my shoulders, all because our common father Adam took a nibble out of an apple tendered by a curvacious spouse (the Baptists have it that it wasn't an apple at all, but that our first parents lay down together and discovered things before they should have). -- "Trouble with you", says my doctor, "is Original Sin and you're going to die -- eventually, anyway." For which he charges me five dollars, currency of the realm. Encore on the Ho hum.

You know it, Johann G., I believe I'm getting old. I gauge this by the tendency to look back, over my shoulder, as it were -- to revive things and incidents that have lain quiescent for decades. I forget what I was doing, or what the weather was like, last Monday; but I vividly recall driving homeward with a load of chopped feed from Gudmundur Davidson's, diagonally across the section east of Julli's at dusk of a November day. A light snow was falling which piled up before the half-sized wheels till they stopped turning but slid runner-wise on the short prairie grass. The phenomenon amazed me, and I stopped to examine whether the wheels had siezed on the axles. -- Things of this nature, mostly unimportant, irrational and inconsequential come back to mind, while incidents of importance, in the sense of changing the current of my life, are bypassed. The little matter of editing over fifteen hundred editions of newspapers over a span of thirty active years in journalism is largely forgotten, but walking the few miles west from Chris. Abrahamson's to Dori Johannesson's at dusk of a winter's day, leaving Joe and Rikka and Valgerdur to proceed home to "Tiu" after a ceremony above a store in Sinclair village, is clearly remembered. Strange, but of no consequence, unless it be that my few years among all you good folk in Pipestone was the stage of my flowering, and so the happiest and most fruitful, however little I realized it at the time. Certainly I look back to that time with more poignant nostalgia than to any other period. -- Julli and Helga, grand people that they were, and are, and how tolerant and understanding they were of my shortcomings; the Abrahamsons, to a man decent and upright, and the rest -- people of truly Good Will and forthright honesty. Later, in the bustle of the market-place, I learned, sometimes the hard way, that such neighborliness is not universal. So, when I hark back, more often it is to Pipestone-byggd and the first decade of the century, and all you good people who figure in it.

Wish I had things to report to you by way of news, but I haven't. Doubtless you know that brother Paul has just issued his second volume of verse. -- Met your bro. Barney at our annual Gooley picnic at Blaine last summer, and greatly enjoyed a lengthy chat with him. -- Looked in on Valgerdur in the early fall, and found everything right-side-up-with-care. -- But mostly things here are on the order of being quiet and sedate, and so of no news value, even to an old "firehorse", a wornout newshound turned out to pasture.

So here's a period to this screed to you, my old and valued friend, with heartiest seasonal greetings and wishes of all the best to you and yours.

Sincerely

BOGI B.

Cultus Lake, BCC.,Canada
January 18, '58

Mr. Yehudi Menuhin
(Address: universal)

Dear Sir.--

Biting my nails that I feel unequal to the journey to
Vancouver for your concerts tomorrow and Tuesday, though I
once travelled much farther to hear you -- to Winnipeg, Manitoba, somewhen in the late thirties, I believe. I found that
experience most worthwhile, for you played some of the works
I had long struggled with, the Mend. E Minor, 64th, for one.
Since first hearing you (on radio from Toronto in the early
thirties), I have numbered you 1 of the current "greats" of
of the violin, followed by Milstein, Heifets, Elman, Fran-
cescatti, Ricci, etc., in that order. -- More power to your
elbow, and as the Scots say, "Lang may yer lum reek!"

On a personal note: My association with the violin
goes 'way back to Joachim, for I studied for some years with
one of his pupils, Herr von Myhr, for someone years concert-
meister of the Berlin Philharmonic, etc., but when I knew
him (1911-on) much the worse for wear -- booze, maybe, although he could at times play like the Master he had once
been. (A German nobleman, he disappeared on outbreak of
WWI, and I have never heard of him since.)

Now a request: -- Please drop me a card with your
permanent home address. I have on "the needles" a short
piece requiring brilliant execution, designed as an en-
core-encore (a sort of period -- that's final), which I
should like to dedicate to you. Will mail a copy to you
if you are further interested.

To reiterate -- Long may your power endure, and the
more you record the better. Count me, a "has-been" and
a "shut-in", as one of your most ardent "fans".

BOGI BJARNASON
(Address above)

Bogi Bjarnason

113 West 57th Street,

New York City.

January 24th.

Dear Mr Bjarnason,

Thank you very much for your kind and flattering letter. How very interesting that you should have studied with a pupil of Jaachim. Just recently I was considering looking at the "Hungarian" concerto and perhaps at the piece for violin and orchestra again, which have long been neglected.

It is very kind of you to wish to dedicate a composition to me. To be absolutely frank, in my appallingly busy life of constant touring and changing of programmes, I cannot ever promise to perform a piece, but if you will accept those conditions, them I shall be highly flattered.

Yours sincerely

Mr Yehudi Menuhin.

Florida.

February 7th.

Dear Mr Bjornason,

    Many thanks for your composition.I take it as a very
kind gesture.
    With best wishes for the best of luck,

        Yours sincerely,

Mr Yehudi Menuhin.

Cultus Lake,B.C.,Canada
July 4, 1958

Dr. Vilhjalmur Stefansson
Hanover, N.H.

Friend V.S.--

In an unguarded moment you wrote on a card to me:
"...Please continue that and every other kind of letter."
That could have its perils for you, considering my vol-
ubility, save only for one thing -- myletters do not call
for replies. Get on with your autobi. *ography*

Were I to attempt to write an autobi. (which heaven
forbid!) I pause to wonder what I would put in it. Looking
back, I seem to remember most clearly the irrelevant, inconsequential things -- riding atop a double-decker wagon
box over a stony trail in southern Sask. on a fall day in
1911, my companion (Joi Davids) tunelessly humming "Meet
Me in St. Louis, Louie", and, about that time, observing a
a phenomenon that for the moment puzzled me. Driving on a
low-wheel wagon, wet-snow falling on short prairie grass,
all four wheels suddenly ceased turning and slid sled-wise,
the snow piling up before them.

I vividly recall sitting in the shade of a stook in
a Saskatchewan wheat field eating the noon-day snack and
discussing with a fellow worker the comparative merits of
Rudyard Kipling and Robert Service rhyming, he favoring the
latter. -- Here let me digress to say that I am reading for
the -th time Kipling's "KIM", even as I periodically reread
"Marjorie Daw" (Henry Bailey Aldritch), and "A Kentucky Cardinal" (James Lane Allen). All have a peculiar fascination
for me. -- Wooing and wedding and raising a family, plung-
ing into various business enterprises, being responsible
for some 2M editions of small-town "rags" in locales where *peop*
wear their sensitivities on their sleeves, equally offended
if you do or do not mention them -- these are in the mists.
Does that make sense!
1

The purpining of a bicycle is clear as day. Let me
tell you about it.

It was somewhen about the turn of the century that a
U.N.D. student, teaching school during the summer recess
uppi a fjöllum (towards Alma, I think), paused hjá Bjarna
og Gróu i Hrisakoti, enroute from Mountain or somewhere
leading a bicycle with a flat tire. He parked his steed behind a shed and made off on foot; he would pick up the bike
come next Friday. -- Came Monday ack emma and Bogi who patch-
ed the puncture and rode off, upp i dal til Fia (son Hall-
dors "Sko" og Olafar), who later married my sister Gunnel.
He had a bicycle, so we made the most of it, exploring the

countryside, Dan to Beersheba (Osnabruck to Gardar), and had
ourelves a glorious time. But on Friday a pedal fell off "my"
bike, the threads gone. With no means of fixing it I sneaked
the bike back behind the shed and disappeared. (Walk away from
a problem and it just disappears!) What the bike's owner
thought of it, and had reason to think, I never learned. I
trust I am forgiven.

Another time --some years before this -- two men came
out of the west, like Lochinvar, on horsebacks driving before
them a herd of untamed horses to be shipped from Canton (later
Hensel). They had been in the saddles all night and probably
the previous day, and the younger of the twain was dog-tired
when they reached the junction between Krossanes and Hrisa-
kot. The hours were still small (4 or 5 a.m.) when he rapped
and was led to bed. The other, an elder brother with hair that
rested on his shoulders, a horseman bred to the saddle, was
eqal to carrying on.

I was routed out (born in Sept., '88, I could have been no
more than 8 or 9) and given a horse and buggy with instructions to drive post haste to Cantonto alert a man there to
make ready a corral to receive the herd. At this point things
become misty, and just don't add up as appear in my mind. I
was to pick up Magnus Bjarnason ("Kripp") at Mountain and take
him with me to Canton. Why, or how this was arranged, is not
clear. But I got to Canton well in time to alert the man of
the corral, after which Magnus canvassed the village with his
wares -- Icelandic books and periodicals. Driving back in the
p.m my little mare being tired began to balk, and west of
Mountain stopped and refused to go on. Along came Arne Sukke,
a farmer on the brow of the hills directly west of Bjargi(on
whose therewas later discovered a valuable deposit of Fullers
Earth),and I hitched on behind him and got home. -- How much
of this right in my mind is not wholly clear to me, but this
is how it emerges.

Of such stuff would be my autobi., rather than recounting how for thirty wearisome years I dealt with news of Mrs.
Brown having members of the WI in for team bridge of a Thurs-
day afternoon, covers being laid for --. "A moulder of public
opinion." My sainted aunt!

That's enogh for the nonce -- no, not quite. Shortly I
shall forward to you a sheaf verses , gathered together from
sundry scrap books. Just don't tell me whether or how you liked them. It's enough that I their worth.

Best wishes

--BOGI B.

Nov. 11, '64

Friend J.P. --

The calendar says Nov. 11, the clock, 11 a.m. I'm on my third

cup of coffee, but still only half-alive, having slept poorly.

An order from the Legion(American) said, "Be at the Cenotaph on

time, to honor our herioc and glorious dead." Being only nine-

tenths dead, I'm not among the "heroic and glorious"; and any-

way, ther's a monstrous hole in my right stocking. Dora is at

Nanaimo (where elder son Don is Social Work superintendent at

Brann Lake School), hailing another gr.-daughter."Eight lbs. and

perfect",says her letter. Well, why shouldn't she be? Look at

her gr.-father. Glory be!!

A look-back says I was in Chatoroux, France, this day in '18,
Anno Domini, being hugged and kissed by innumerable distaff side
namsels, who no doubt liked my (American) uniform better than
my phiz. I was a "hero", having won the war, and survived, after
a fashion. I had been not quite scared to death, however nearly,
and so a "hero". God save the mark! So I'm not at the cenotaph as
ordered, but at the typewriter (the clock says precisely 11), 46
years later, pecking this out, one finger. Not yet quite dead.

Still looking back to those far days. A few days after the gruel-
ling St. Mihiel "show" we we shifted to the Argonne, foot-slog-
ging under 100-lb. (believe it or not) packs. On the morning of
Sept. 26 (my 30th birthday) we went "over the top" after a twelve
hour march in the rain (during which I came nearest to losing my
precious life by reason of breaking out a meat-sandwich I had
saved at suppertime (I had not been warned that it was all but a
capital offence to eat on a march, for a good reason). During
the next three days Co.E 2nd Batt. 35th Div. Kansas-Missouri advanced from Exermont along the Aire past Verdun to Exermont, sup
ported by Capt. Harry S. Truman's 6th Field Artillery, whose
shells more than once fell short (as I was to tell him later in
correspondence). That Major Reiger, whose runner and "dog-Robber
I was, was just as scared as myself, supported me, and we collapsed all but together, spent. That he finished as Colonel and I
private 1st Class means much or little; I don't know. God knows
I was not "brave", nor was Reiger. The two Jerrys who held up
their hands to me (I still have the correspondence and "Goot-Mit
Uns"/ belt of one) were no braver. They wanted to be taken pris-

oner. I did not want their lives, nor, I felt, they mine. But
Pres. Wilson sent me an "accolade" and said/ was a hero, and
to this day a generous U.S. Vet. Administration sends me a
cheque every moth (not very big, having only been a private),
for what, I don't know. They paid me a dollar a day "and found"
for just/ tagging along. I spent a lot of ammunition, to no
purpose that I could see, other than to get rid of the weight.
So to speak, I never saw a German (other than prisoners), and
would probably have turned tail had I seen a bayonet coming at
me. But Wilson said I was a hero (I have it in writing). What
a Hero! -- And what would we do without wars, and rumors of
wars? I ask you.

On this day (it's now well past 11 a.m.) when I should have been
down at the cenotaph "honoring the dead") my mind goes back to
Chatoroux and the bedlam that evening of Nov. 11, '18 (A.D.).
Not a few of my/ buddies ended up in bordellos (freely advertised as such). Whatever France is like now, to me it was a bit
shocking then, what little I saw. I still recall entering a
little shop, where vin rouge sold for 10¢ a (big) bottle (vin
blanc, much stronger), 20¢. A rack of post-cards depicting all
the possible positions of coitus was presided over by a nice
looking girl saying "ooh-la-la". Price (of cards) 2 for 5¢.
Well, some water has passed over the dam since then; but I am
told that to this day you can stand against a wall anywher in
Paris and relieve yourself without exciting comment. They have
probably never heard of the dictum I Kings, 14, verse 10. Anyway, who cares?

Joe -- I often feel these days that I have'nt far to go, which
does't distress me at all. 76 plus is a fair span. Why should I
continue to clutter up the works, to no purpose? I tried to get
this across to thr two nice-looking women, Jehovah's Witnesses,
who came to my door to tell me that Armageddon (or something)
was all but here. When I told them I wouldn't go across the
street to witness the end of the world, nor even to the curb to
shake hands with Jesus Christ, they left shaking their heads.
I'm lost, said their attitude. Could be. -- Half eviscerated,
after six (6) major operations, what I want now is OUT, and not
to wake up. I want to see neither Helen in Hell nor Knox in Paradise. Vale.

      1
Fyrirgefdu maegina

                                        BOGI

3391 West 20th Ave., Van.
Nov. 12, '64

Dear Joe,--

Middle of last night (when I'm most awake) got to thinking back
to
'18 and Argonne, mentioned in a note to you yesterday. I was

younger then (age 30), which makes a difference. I could sleep

on the ground, cold feet and all, hungry and scared and miser-

able. Now I lie awake in a comfortable bed, with nothing more

formidable ahead than a bill from B.C. Hydro. Does that make

sense? In 76 years I haven't learned much.

In the fall of '18 I was Major Reiger's "dogrobber" (batman),
Runner was the designation, which meant that I put up his pup-
tent and dug his individual straddle-ditch (though he never required that I wipe him). A lawyer and Sunday school teacher in
civil life he was, in his way, yet a gentleman, however conscious he was of the tremendous gap between officer and private.
I tried to see, and respect, that, but found it hard, brought up
as I was in the sticks of No. Dak. and in the shadow of Vikur
kirkju, having never seen my country's military uniform till in
my majority. Once in his tent when I was tucking him in he un-
bent a little, saying that he prayed before sleep, and that King
David was his ideal soldier. I thought of pointing out to him
1 Sam., ch. 27, verse 9 (which see) but didn't. I could also have
pointed to II Sam. ch. 12, verse 31, but didn't. I was the ideal
"Yes, Sir" man. ------

Hiatus here - a nap after soup. Why do I sleep better in bright
daylight than in the dead of night? You're a doctor, so send me
a bill. I'll probably send it back with a notation: "Go to hell".
You mustn't take umbrage. It's just Bogi sounding off.

But getting back to Reiger and the Argonne. Corresponding with
him back in Kelvington dys, when I had in mind writing a book
about my war experiences, I asked him, "Did you say that?" "If
I did, don't quote me." But I had heard him say it. "Kill the
bastards; that's what you're here for." -- When I was assigned
to him he said, "Don't ever address me, save through the sergeant; don't even look at me, and stand at attention." Which
meant, You're in the army, and I'm an officer." Almighty God!

Reiger, lawyer and Sunday-school teacher, in his way a gentleman, if in uniform a martinet, had his weak moments. I learned
that on our second out from Vauquois Hill when a shell-splinter
hurt his hand. "That could have hit my face, or liver, as well."
He didn't ask to be relieved; but I felt that he was just as
scared as I, which was plenty. -- Back at Metzeral I thought I
had seen the ultimate lunacy of war. I hadn't. The 26th - 30 of
Sept., Anno Domini '18, were worse. On the 30th I collapsed.
But to this day that time is with me, mostly at night. I just
cant get rid of it, or of Reiger.

Why am I writing this to you? -- This p.m. Barney Bjornson and
Kelly Sveinsson (Valdi's brother) looked in on me, both look-
ing very despite high age. I could have asked them, but didn't.
The '14-'18 war is over, except for me. How do I get rid of it?

Encore, fyrirgefdu maegina.

                                                    BOGI B.

    Short of the fee-at-hand
    For my eternal keep,
    Lord, grant me at the end
    The gift of sleep.

- - 30 - -

(The End)